This book is presented for educational and personal development purposes.

ISBN: 9798253594148

Printed in the United States of America

To my son **Kai**,
whose life and memory revealed the deepest truth within my experience.

To my daughter **Isabella**,
whose presence reminds me of the beauty of life.

To my other half **Elif**,
for her love, patience, and support.

To my family, friends, and all the people who have influenced my journey.

And most of all,

To **the one and only God of all creation**,
for allowing me to experience this world.

Sadness is the expectation
for the circumstance
to be different than it actually is.

Expectation creates conditions.

When those conditions are not satisfied,
suffering appears.

But when expectation dissolves,
something else becomes visible.

Peace.

True peace is attained through
the recognition of your choice.

Experiology

Experiology *(noun)*
ex·pe·ri·ol·o·gy /ikˌspirēˈäləjē/

Formal Definition

Experiology is the interdisciplinary study of how human beings gain awareness, understanding, and truth through lived experience and reflective choice.

It examines how emotions, perceptions, and life events reveal underlying expectations and provide opportunities for conscious decision-making that leads to greater awareness and personal transformation.

Expanded Definition

Experiology proposes that experience itself is a teaching mechanism. Through reflection on emotions and circumstances, individuals are able to recognize the choices they are making and develop greater awareness of themselves and their relationship to reality.

Within Experiology, emotions are understood as signals that reveal the expectations a person holds about life. By recognizing these expectations, individuals can consciously choose how they respond to experience.

The discipline therefore focuses on the development of awareness through the application of seven foundational attributes:

- Purpose
- Thankfulness
- Intention
- Acceptance
- Understanding
- Forgiveness
- Unconditional Love

Through the integration of these attributes, a person moves from resistance toward awareness, ultimately resulting in peace.

Core Principle of Experiology

The central principle of Experiology is that awareness develops through experience.

Life continually presents experiences that evoke emotion. These emotions reveal the expectations we hold about reality. When individuals reflect on these expectations, they begin to recognize the perceptions shaping their understanding of the world.

Through this process, a deeper realization appears.

Human beings possess the ability to consciously choose how they respond to experience.

This moment of recognition reveals that awareness is not something given to us automatically. It emerges when we become conscious of our expectations and reflect on the emotions they produce.

In that moment, we discover our ability to choose understanding rather than resistance.

Experiology therefore recognizes that experience is not merely something that happens to us. Experience is the mechanism through which awareness becomes possible.

The core realization of Experiology can be expressed simply:

Human existence is the opportunity to choose awareness through experience.

Foundational Insight

A central realization within Experiology is that emotional suffering often arises when reality does not match the expectations we hold.

Human beings naturally form expectations about how circumstances should unfold. When those expectations conflict with reality, emotional discomfort appears. This discomfort may be experienced as sadness, frustration, resentment, or grief.

Through reflection on emotion, individuals begin to recognize the expectation that produced it.

This realization can be expressed simply:

Sadness is the expectation for the circumstance to be different than it actually is.

When this expectation becomes visible, something important happens.

We recognize that the emotion itself is not the problem. Instead, the emotion reveals the expectation we are holding about reality.

In that moment of recognition, awareness begins.

And with awareness comes the realization that we have a choice in how we respond to the experience before us.

Through this recognition, individuals begin to move from resistance toward understanding.

From that understanding, the pathway of awareness becomes clear.

How to Use This Book

This book is not meant to be read only once.

It is meant to be **observed through your own experience**.

The Seven Attributes describe a process that occurs within the mind when we encounter life's circumstances. As you read, take time to reflect on the ideas presented and notice how they appear within your own thoughts, emotions, and expectations.

The attributes described in this book are:

Purpose
Thankfulness
Intention
Acceptance
Understanding
Forgiveness
Unconditional Love

These attributes represent the movement of awareness toward peace.

At the same time, each attribute has a reflection that appears when expectation and resistance remain present:

No Purpose
Conditional Thankfulness
Ill Intention
Denial
Not Understanding
Not Forgiving
Conditional Love

As you move through the chapters, you may begin to notice moments in your own life where awareness shifts between these two directions.

The diagrams included in this book—such as the **Seven Attributes Model**, the **Awareness Spiral**, and the **Resistance vs Awareness chart**—are designed to help visualize these patterns.

You do not need to understand everything immediately.

Simply read with curiosity and honesty.

The most important question you can ask yourself as you read is simple:

What expectation am I holding right now?

When that question is asked honestly, the process of self-awareness begins to reveal itself.

And when awareness appears, something else becomes visible.

The choice.

Table of Contents

Front Matter

Experiology

Part I — The Realization

Part II — The Experiology Framework

Part III — The Seven Attributes

Part IV — Awareness Through Experience

Part V — Living the Awareness

Part VI — The Experiology Models

Closing Section

Back Matter

I — The Realization

CHAPTER 1

Introduction — The Question

There are moments in life when a single question changes everything.

Not a question asked out of curiosity, but one asked out of deep necessity. A question born from experience. A question that refuses to leave until it is answered.

For me, that question came from grief.

My sister had died, and I found myself in a place many people know but few truly understand. It was not just sadness. It was something deeper—an overwhelming weight that seemed impossible to escape. A feeling that sat heavy in the chest and lingered in the mind.

In that moment, I asked a question that would begin a journey of discovery:

What is grief?

What is sorrow?
What is sadness?
Where does it come from?

Most people believe emotions are caused by the world around them. They believe circumstances create their feelings. If something painful happens, sadness simply follows.

But what if that assumption is incomplete?

What if emotions are not simply reactions to the world, but signals revealing something deeper about how we relate to it?

As I searched for the answer, a realization slowly emerged:

Sadness is the expectation for the circumstance to be different than it actually is.

At first, this realization was only an idea. It made sense intellectually, but it had not yet been fully tested.

That test would come later.

When my son died, I encountered the greatest emotional experience a human being can face. Deep grief. Deep sorrow. Deep sadness.

And yet, within that moment of pain, something profound happened.

I remembered the question I had once asked.

What is grief?

What is sadness?

And in that moment, the answer was no longer theoretical. It became real through experience.

I saw clearly that my suffering came from a single condition within my mind: the expectation that the circumstance should be different than it was.

I wanted reality to change.

I wanted the moment to be something other than what it was.

But reality does not change to satisfy expectation.

It simply is.

In that realization, something shifted.

Instead of focusing on the time I no longer had with my son, I became thankful for the time I had been given. I became thankful that I had been able to experience his life, his presence, and the love that existed between us.

That thankfulness had no condition.

It did not depend on circumstances being different.

It was simply appreciation for what had been experienced.

And in that moment, grief gave way to something else.

Unconditional love.

This experience revealed a deeper truth about human awareness: emotions are not random occurrences. They arise from the way we interpret our experiences.

If we hold expectations and conditions, suffering appears.

If we accept reality and become thankful for what is, peace becomes possible.

From this realization emerged a framework that explains how the mind moves between resistance and peace.

This framework is what I call **The Seven Attributes to Self-Awareness**.

These seven attributes describe the process through which human beings experience emotion, make meaning of their circumstances, and ultimately arrive at one of two outcomes: resistance or acceptance.

When understood and applied together, they lead to a single realization:

True peace is attained only through the recognition of your choice.

The question is not whether life will present challenges.

The question is whether we will recognize the choice available within every experience.

And perhaps the most important question of all is this:

Will you be honest with yourself about the choice you are making?

CHAPTER 2

The Realization

Every meaningful discovery begins with an experience that forces a person to question what they thought they understood.

For most of my life, emotions seemed like something that simply happened to me. Like most people, I believed that circumstances created my feelings. When something good happened, I felt happiness. When something painful happened, I felt sadness. It appeared natural and unavoidable.

But the experience of grief forced me to look deeper.

After the death of my sister, I found myself sitting with a feeling that felt endless. It was heavy and consuming. It was not just sadness—it was something deeper, something that seemed to pull the mind constantly back into the past.

That was when the question first appeared:

What is grief?

I did not ask the question casually. I asked it because the weight of the experience demanded an answer.

I wanted to understand where the feeling came from. Was grief something imposed on us by life, or was it something created within the mind?

As I began reflecting on the experience, a realization slowly began to form.

Grief did not come from the event itself.

It came from the mind's relationship to the event.

The mind wanted the circumstance to be different than it actually was. It wanted the moment to reverse. It wanted reality to change.

And when reality did not change, the mind resisted it.

That resistance created the emotional weight we call grief.

From this observation came a simple but profound realization:
Sadness is the expectation for the circumstance to be different than it actually is.

This understanding revealed something deeper about human experience.

Emotions are not simply reactions to events. They are reflections of how we interpret those events.

When the mind holds expectations or conditions that reality does not satisfy, resistance appears. That resistance creates emotions such as sadness, resentment, anger, or grief.

In other words, many of the emotions we struggle with are not created by life itself. They are created by the conditions we place on life.

This realization was powerful, but at the time it was still only an idea. I had not yet been forced to fully apply it.

That moment would come later.

When my son died, I experienced grief again—but this time it was deeper than anything I had ever known.

The pain was immense.
But something had changed.

Within the experience, I remembered the realization that had come years earlier.

I remembered the question.

What is grief?

And in that moment, I could see clearly what was happening inside my own mind.

Part of me wanted reality to be different. Part of me wanted the circumstance to change. I wanted more time. I wanted the moment to reverse.

Those desires created the weight of grief.

But another choice was also available.

I could recognize the expectation itself.

I could see the condition my mind was placing on reality.

And I could release it.

Instead of focusing on what I no longer had, I could recognize what I had already experienced.

I had been given the opportunity to know my son. I had experienced his presence, his life, and the love that existed between us.

When I shifted my perspective in that way, something remarkable happened.

Grief no longer dominated the experience.

What remained was love.

Not conditional love based on what I wished had happened.

But **unconditional love for the experience itself**.

I became thankful—not because the circumstance was easy, but because the experience had been real.

This moment revealed something profound.

Peace does not come from controlling life.

Peace comes from recognizing the choice we have in how we relate to life.

That realization became the foundation for the framework that would eventually emerge as **The Seven Attributes to Self-Awareness**.

Each attribute represents a stage in the way human beings process experience.

Together, they reveal the path from resistance to awareness.

And at the center of that path lies the most important realization of all:

We always have a choice.

The moment we recognize that choice, awareness begins.

And when awareness is fully realized, something extraordinary becomes possible.

Peace.

CHAPTER 3

What Is Sadness?

Sadness is one of the most common emotions experienced by human beings, yet very few people stop to ask what it actually is.

Most people assume sadness is caused by circumstances. When something painful happens, sadness follows. When something is lost, sadness appears. Because this pattern seems consistent, it is easy to believe that the event itself creates the emotion.

But this assumption overlooks something important.

If sadness were caused purely by circumstances, then every person experiencing the same situation would feel sadness in the same way. Yet this is clearly not the case. Two people can experience the same event and respond completely differently.

One person may remain peaceful while another becomes overwhelmed with grief.

Why?
The answer lies not in the event itself, but in the interpretation of the event.

Through reflection and experience, a simple realization emerges:

Sadness is the expectation for the circumstance to be different than it actually is.

At its core, sadness is not simply an emotional reaction. It is a signal that the mind is holding an expectation that reality has not satisfied.

The mind imagines how things should be. It creates a preferred version of reality. When the real circumstance does not match that expectation, resistance appears.

That resistance is experienced as sadness.

In this way, sadness is not created by life itself.

It is created by the conditions we place on life.

When the mind says:

This should not have happened.

or

Things should be different than they are.

it creates a conflict between expectation and reality.

That conflict produces emotional tension.

Sadness is the experience of that tension.

This does not mean that sadness is wrong or unnatural. In fact, sadness serves an important purpose. It reveals when the mind is holding onto an expectation that reality cannot fulfill.

In other words, sadness is not a problem to solve.

It is information.

It is a signal pointing toward something happening within the mind.

Once this is understood, sadness begins to look different.

Instead of viewing sadness as something imposed upon us, we begin to see it as a reflection of our relationship with reality.

This realization opens the door to a deeper question:

If sadness comes from expectation, what happens when expectation is released?

When the mind stops demanding that circumstances be different than they are, resistance disappears.

And when resistance disappears, something unexpected takes its place.

Acceptance.

Acceptance does not mean that difficult experiences become easy. It means we stop fighting reality itself.

When acceptance is present, the mind becomes free from the tension created by unmet expectations.

From acceptance, a new possibility emerges.

Thankfulness.

Not conditional thankfulness based on circumstances being perfect, but **thankfulness for the experience itself**.

This shift marks the beginning of a deeper understanding of human awareness.

Sadness reveals the expectation.

Acceptance releases the expectation.

And thankfulness opens the door to something greater.

The path continues from there.

But it begins with recognizing the truth hidden within a simple question:

What is sadness?

CHAPTER 4

Expectation and Emotion

Expectation

The Standard of Experience

Every human experience begins with expectation.

Expectation is the internal standard a person holds about how something **should happen**, **might happen**, or **must happen**. These standards are rarely spoken aloud, yet they shape how every event in life is interpreted.

Expectations are formed through many sources: past experiences, beliefs, cultural norms, personal values, and assumptions about how the world works. Over time these elements build an internal framework that predicts what reality should look like.

Because of this, expectation acts as the **reference point for experience**.

When an event occurs, the mind automatically compares reality to the expectation that already exists. This comparison happens almost instantly and often outside of conscious awareness.

Expectation therefore does not simply predict experience—it **defines the standard by which experience will be judged**.

A person who expects respect will evaluate interactions differently than someone who expects rejection. A person who expects failure will interpret outcomes differently than someone who expects success.

The external event may be the same, yet the experience of that event can be entirely different depending on the expectation that preceded it.

In Experiology, expectation is recognized as the **first attribute of experience**, because every emotional reaction begins with this comparison between expectation and reality.

Without expectation there is no standard, and without a standard there is no emotional signal to interpret the outcome.

Expectation establishes the starting point of the experiential cycle.

Emotion

The Signal of Experience

Emotion is the signal that arises when reality is measured against expectation.

While emotions are often treated as causes of behavior, Experiology recognizes them as **information**. Emotion communicates the result of the comparison between what was expected and what actually occurred.

When reality exceeds expectation, emotions such as excitement, joy, or relief may arise. When reality meets expectation, a sense of stability or satisfaction may occur. When reality violates expectation, emotions such as frustration, sadness, fear, or anger may appear.

In this way emotion acts as a **messenger**, informing the individual that a meaningful difference has occurred between expectation and reality.

Emotion therefore serves an important purpose: it draws attention to experience.

Rather than being something to suppress or eliminate, emotion is the mechanism through which experience becomes noticeable. It signals that something important has occurred and that interpretation is about to follow.

This is why emotions are powerful—they indicate that the mind is preparing to assign meaning to what has just happened.

Within the Experiology framework, emotions exist for a deeper purpose:

Emotions exist so that a person can experience choice.

The emotional signal creates awareness. Awareness creates the opportunity to interpret experience. Interpretation leads to choice.

Emotion is therefore not the end of experience—it is the **gateway that leads to conscious decision-making**.

In the cycle of the Seven Attributes, emotion moves the individual toward the next stage: perception.

The Transition Between Expectation and Emotion in the Wheel

The movement from expectation to emotion represents the first shift within the cycle of human experience.

Expectation exists before the event occurs. It establishes the internal prediction of how reality should unfold.

When reality appears, the mind immediately performs a comparison between what was expected and what actually happened. This comparison happens automatically and often outside conscious awareness.

Emotion emerges as the signal produced by this comparison.

This moment—the instant where expectation meets reality—is where experience truly begins.

The wheel of the Seven Attributes captures this movement. Expectation sets the standard. Emotion communicates the result of that standard being tested against reality.

The emotional signal then directs attention toward understanding the event. From there the mind begins to organize what happened through perception, eventually assigning meaning, making choices, taking action, and observing results.

Once results are experienced, they influence future expectations, and the cycle begins again.

Through this continuous loop, humans are constantly interpreting reality and shaping future expectations through experience.

The wheel therefore represents not just a model of behavior, but the **living structure of how experience unfolds**.

CHAPTER 5

The Moment of Choice

Every experience contains a moment that is easy to miss.

It is brief, often unnoticed, and yet it determines the direction of everything that follows.

This is the **moment of choice**.

After an event occurs, the mind compares what happened with what was expected. When the two do not match, emotion appears. Emotion signals that something meaningful has taken place.

At that moment, most people believe the emotion itself is controlling them. They feel anger, sadness, or frustration and assume the emotion is forcing their reaction.

But emotion is not the force that determines behavior.

Emotion is the **signal that a choice is now available**.

Between the emotional signal and the action that follows, there exists a small but powerful space. In that space, the individual can decide how to interpret what has happened and how they will respond to it.

This space is the moment of choice.

Many people move through this moment without noticing it. Their reactions are automatic, shaped by habits and past experiences. The emotion appears, and the response follows almost immediately.

Yet awareness reveals that this sequence is not fixed.

When a person recognizes the emotional signal, they can pause long enough to see the choice that is present. They can decide whether to react in the familiar way or to respond with greater awareness.

This is where personal power exists.

Choice does not erase the emotion, nor does it deny the experience. Instead, it allows the individual to decide what meaning they will give to what has happened and what action they will take moving forward.

In this sense, emotion is not an obstacle to awareness. It is the doorway that leads to it.

Emotion announces that something important has occurred. Awareness reveals that a choice is now possible.

The moment a person recognizes this, experience begins to change.

Life is no longer something that simply happens to them. Instead, each experience becomes an opportunity to respond consciously.

This realization forms the foundation of Experiology.

Because once a person understands that emotion signals the presence of choice, they begin to see experience differently. Events are no longer just reactions waiting to happen. They are invitations to awareness.

Every experience contains a moment of choice.

And within that moment lies the possibility of living with greater understanding, clarity, and peace.

Part II — The Experiology Framework

CHAPTER 6

The Experiology Framework

Every moment of life is an experience.

Yet most people move through experience without ever examining how it unfolds. Events occur, emotions arise, reactions follow, and life continues forward. Because this process happens continuously, it often appears automatic.

Experiology proposes that experience is not random. It follows a structure that can be understood.

This structure is known as **The Experiology Framework**.

The framework describes the internal movement that occurs whenever something happens in a person's life. It reveals how an external event becomes an internal experience and how that experience ultimately leads to action.

The framework consists of four stages:

Experience
Emotion
Reflection
Choice

Each stage plays a specific role in the development of awareness.

First, something happens in the external world. A conversation, a thought, a memory, or an event enters a person's awareness. This is the moment of **experience**.

Next, the mind compares what has occurred with its expectations. If there is a difference between what was expected and what actually happened, an emotional signal appears. This is **emotion**.

Emotion then invites the next stage, which is **reflection**. Reflection allows the person to examine the experience, consider its meaning, and understand why the emotional signal appeared.

Finally, reflection leads to **choice**. Once awareness is present, the individual has the ability to decide how they will respond.

This sequence is constantly repeating in every person's life. It operates in simple moments and in profound ones. It occurs during conversations, during conflicts, during joy, and during difficulty.

Most of the time this cycle happens so quickly that it is barely noticed.

Experiology does not attempt to stop the cycle. Instead, it helps a person become aware of it.

When someone begins to recognize these stages within their own experiences, something important happens. They discover that between emotion and action there is space.

Within that space exists the possibility of awareness.

And within awareness exists the ability to choose.

CHAPTER 7

Experience

Everything begins with experience.

Experience is the moment when reality enters awareness. It is the point where life presents itself to the individual through events, interactions, thoughts, and sensations.

An experience may be something external, such as a conversation, a situation, or an unexpected event. It may also be internal, such as a memory, an idea, or a thought that suddenly arises.

Regardless of its origin, experience is the doorway through which life becomes known.

Most people assume that experiences themselves determine how they feel. If something pleasant happens, they expect to feel good. If something unpleasant occurs, they expect to feel bad.

Experiology suggests that the situation is more complex.

Events alone do not determine emotional reactions. Instead, experiences interact with expectations that already exist within the mind.

The meaning a person assigns to an event depends largely on what they believed would happen before the event occurred.

For this reason, two individuals can encounter the same situation and experience it very differently.

One person may see opportunity where another sees loss. One may interpret an event as rejection while another interprets it as feedback.

The external experience may be identical, yet the internal experience can vary greatly.

Understanding this distinction is important.

Experience is not only what happens in the world. It is the moment where the world and the individual meet.

It is the beginning of the internal process that eventually leads to emotion, reflection, and choice.

CHAPTER 8

Emotion

Emotion is the signal that follows experience.

When something occurs, the mind automatically compares the event with its expectations. If the event differs from what was anticipated, an emotional signal appears.

Emotion therefore serves as a form of internal communication. It informs the individual that something significant has taken place.

This signal may appear as joy, sadness, frustration, excitement, fear, or many other emotional states. Each emotion communicates that the mind has detected a meaningful difference between expectation and reality.

Because emotions can feel intense, many people assume that emotions control their behavior. They believe that anger forces them to react or that sadness prevents them from moving forward.

Experiology offers a different perspective.

Emotion does not control behavior. Instead, emotion provides **information**.

It tells the individual that the experience they are encountering deserves attention.

Emotion highlights the moment where awareness is needed.

Rather than being something to avoid or suppress, emotion becomes an invitation to look more closely at the experience that has occurred.

In this way emotion plays a crucial role within the framework.

Without emotion, many experiences would pass unnoticed. Emotion brings them into focus and signals that reflection is needed.

CHAPTER 9

Reflection

Reflection is the stage where awareness begins.

After emotion signals that something meaningful has occurred, the individual has the opportunity to pause and examine the experience. Reflection allows a person to step back from the immediate emotional reaction and consider what is actually happening.

During reflection, questions naturally arise:

Why did this experience affect me the way it did?
What expectation was involved?
What meaning am I assigning to this situation?

Reflection transforms emotion from a reaction into an opportunity for understanding.

Instead of being overwhelmed by emotion, the individual becomes curious about it. They begin to observe their thoughts, assumptions, and interpretations.

This process deepens awareness.

Through reflection, a person begins to see the patterns that shape their experiences.

They may notice expectations they were not previously aware of. They may recognize beliefs that influence how they interpret events.

Reflection therefore acts as the bridge between emotion and conscious action.

Without reflection, emotions often lead directly to reaction. With reflection, emotions lead to awareness.

And awareness prepares the mind for the final stage of the framework.

CHAPTER 10

Choice

Choice is the point where awareness becomes action.

After reflecting on an experience, the individual arrives at a moment where a response must be decided. This moment is the place where the direction of experience can change.

Choice determines how the individual will move forward.

They may choose to react in the same way they always have, reinforcing familiar patterns of behavior. Or they may choose a different response, one that reflects greater awareness and understanding.

This is the point where personal responsibility becomes visible.

Experiology does not suggest that people can control every event that occurs in their lives. Experiences will continue to arise in ways that cannot always be predicted.

However, the framework reveals that individuals do have influence over how they respond to those experiences.

Choice is where that influence exists.

Every moment of reflection leads to a decision, whether it is made consciously or unconsciously. By becoming aware of this moment, a person gains the ability to shape their actions rather than simply reacting to circumstances.

Choice therefore represents the culmination of the Experiology Framework.

Experience introduces the event.
Emotion signals its significance.
Reflection brings awareness.
Choice determines the response.

And once a choice is made, the cycle begins again as new experiences unfold.

What makes this choice visible is awareness.

When awareness begins to observe the movements of the mind, it starts to notice something else that is equally important.

Every path toward awareness has an opposite direction.

Every attribute that leads toward peace has a reflection that leads toward resistance.

Understanding this reflection reveals the two directions the mind can move within any experience.

CHAPTER 11

The Reflection

Once the process of awareness becomes visible, something else begins to appear.

Every attribute that leads toward awareness also has a reflection.

This reflection represents the opposite direction the mind can move when expectation and condition remain in control.

In other words, the Seven Attributes do not exist alone.

They exist alongside their opposites.

These opposites form what can be called the reflection of awareness.

When awareness is present, the mind moves through the attributes toward peace.

When awareness is absent, the mind moves through their reflections toward resistance.

The reflections appear as follows:

Purpose reflects **no purpose.**

Thankfulness reflects **conditional thankfulness.**

Intention reflects **ill intention.**

Acceptance reflects **denial.**

Understanding reflects **not understanding.**

Forgiveness reflects **not forgiving.**

Unconditional love reflects **conditional love.**

These reflections reveal something important about human experience.

At every stage of awareness, a choice exists.

For example, when a person encounters a difficult experience, they may recognize that the experience has purpose.

Or they may believe it has no purpose at all.

When something painful happens, they may become thankful for the time they were given.

Or they may become resentful that circumstances did not satisfy their expectations.

The same pattern appears at every level of the process.

A person can move toward goodwill, or toward ill intention.

Toward acceptance, or toward denial.

Toward understanding, or toward confusion.

Toward forgiveness, or toward resentment.

Toward unconditional love, or toward conditional love.

These reflections do not represent separate systems.

They represent two directions the mind can move through the same experience.

One direction leads toward resistance.

The other leads toward awareness.

This is why the Seven Attributes function together as a process rather than isolated ideas.

They reveal the path awareness takes when the mind recognizes the truth of its own choices.

When awareness is present, the attributes align and guide the mind toward peace.

When awareness is absent, the reflections dominate and the mind becomes trapped in cycles of expectation and resistance.

Seeing this reflection clearly is an important step in self-awareness.

It allows a person to observe where their mind is moving in any given moment.

Instead of feeling lost in emotion, they can recognize the direction their awareness is taking.

Are they moving toward resentment or thankfulness?

Toward denial or acceptance?

Toward confusion or understanding?

Toward resentment or forgiveness?

Each moment reveals the answer.

And each moment presents a new opportunity to choose the direction awareness will move.

This reflection shows something powerful about human consciousness.

Life constantly presents experiences.

But the direction those experiences take within us depends on something deeper.

It depends on the choice we make in how we relate to them.

Once this becomes visible, awareness grows.

And as awareness grows, the process becomes easier to recognize.

The Seven Attributes begin to function not just as ideas, but as a guide for understanding the movements of the mind.

They show us the difference between resistance and peace.

And they remind us of the simple truth at the center of every experience:

We always have a choice.

When these reflections dominate awareness, the mind becomes trapped in resistance.

But when the attributes guide awareness instead, something very different begins to appear.

Peace.

Understanding the difference between resistance and awareness reveals how peace becomes possible within experience.

CHAPTER 12

Peace

When a person begins to understand the Seven Attributes, something important becomes visible.

Life itself does not guarantee peace.

Circumstances change.
Loss occurs.
Unexpected events appear.

No human life unfolds exactly as expected.

For many people, peace becomes something they wait for. They believe peace will arrive when life becomes easier, when problems disappear, or when circumstances finally align with their expectations.

But through the process of awareness, a different truth emerges.

Peace is not something created by circumstances.

Peace is created by the relationship we have with circumstances.

When the mind holds expectations that reality must satisfy, peace becomes fragile.

It depends on events unfolding exactly the way we want them to.

When those expectations are not fulfilled, resistance appears, and peace disappears.

But when expectations are released, something changes.

The mind no longer depends on life behaving in a particular way in order to remain calm.

Instead of fighting reality, it begins to move with it.

This movement is what the Seven Attributes describe.

Purpose allows us to see meaning within experience.

Thankfulness allows us to appreciate what has been given.

Intention guides our awareness toward goodwill.

Acceptance releases the struggle against reality.

Understanding reveals the role of expectation and choice.

Forgiveness frees us from the weight of the past.

And unconditional love becomes the center of awareness.

When these attributes begin to align, peace naturally appears.

Peace is not something forced.

It is the natural result of awareness.

When expectation dissolves, resistance fades.

When resistance fades, the mind becomes quiet.

And in that quiet space, peace reveals itself.

This peace does not mean life becomes free of difficulty.

Challenges will still occur.

Loss will still exist.

But awareness changes the way we experience those moments.

Instead of being overwhelmed by them, we see them clearly.

We recognize that every experience still contains the same opportunity that has always existed.

The opportunity to choose.

Peace comes from recognizing that choice.

It comes from understanding that while we may not control the events of life, we always participate in the meaning those events hold within us.

When this realization becomes clear, something remarkable happens.

The search for peace ends.

Not because life has become perfect, but because we have learned how to live within it without demanding that it be different than it is.

And in that moment, the truth at the center of the Seven Attributes becomes unmistakable.

True peace is attained through the recognition of your choice.

The question that remains is simple.

Will you be honest with yourself about the choice you are making?

Part III — The Seven Attributes

CHAPTER 13

Purpose

Once a person begins to see that sadness comes from expectation and condition, another question naturally appears:

Is there a purpose in experience?

When difficult events occur, the mind often assumes they are meaningless or unfair. Painful circumstances can feel random, and when viewed through the lens of expectation, they appear only as loss.

But when expectation is examined more closely, a different possibility begins to emerge.

What if experiences are not simply things that happen to us?

What if they are opportunities to understand something deeper about ourselves?

This shift in perspective introduces the concept of **purpose**.

Purpose does not mean that every event is designed in advance or that suffering exists for a predetermined reason. Instead, purpose refers to the meaning we discover through our experience.

When we encounter difficulty, we are presented with a choice. We can interpret the experience as meaningless and resist it, or we can ask what the experience reveals about our relationship with reality.

Purpose appears when we begin asking that question.

Through reflection, many people eventually notice that the most challenging experiences in their lives often reveal the greatest insights. Difficult moments force the mind to confront assumptions it once believed were unquestionable.

They reveal expectations.

They expose conditions.

And they create the opportunity to recognize something that is normally hidden:

our ability to choose how we respond.

In this way, purpose is not something imposed on life from the outside. It is something discovered through awareness.

When we recognize purpose in our experiences, even painful ones begin to look different. They become teachers rather than enemies.

Instead of asking:

Why did this happen to me?

we begin asking:

What can I learn from this experience?

This question does not erase the reality of difficulty, but it changes the relationship we have with it.

Purpose transforms experience from something we resist into something we can understand.

Once purpose is recognized, another transformation becomes possible.

Instead of seeing life only through the lens of loss or unfairness, the mind begins to notice something else:

the opportunity to appreciate what has been given.

This is where the next attribute begins to emerge.

Thankfulness.

Thankfulness grows naturally when purpose is recognized. When we see that experience can teach us something meaningful, gratitude begins to replace resentment.

In this way, purpose becomes the doorway that leads the mind away from resistance and toward awareness.

It is the first step in recognizing that every experience contains the possibility of understanding.

And that understanding begins with a simple realization:

Life may not always meet our expectations, but every experience still has the potential to reveal something valuable.

CHAPTER 14

Thankfulness

Once a person begins to recognize purpose within their experiences, something important begins to change in the way the mind relates to life.

Instead of seeing events only through the lens of loss or unfairness, the mind begins to notice what has been given.

This shift introduces the next attribute in the process of awareness:

Thankfulness.

Thankfulness is often misunderstood. Many people believe gratitude should only appear when circumstances are favorable. When life goes well, thankfulness feels natural. But when life becomes difficult, gratitude can seem impossible.

This is because most people practice what could be called **conditional thankfulness**.

Conditional thankfulness depends on circumstances meeting certain expectations. It appears only when life unfolds in the way we hoped it would.

When conditions are satisfied, gratitude arises.

When conditions are not satisfied, resentment appears instead.

This form of thankfulness is unstable because it relies entirely on external events.

But there is another form of gratitude that exists beyond circumstance.

This is **unconditional thankfulness**.

Unconditional thankfulness does not depend on life being perfect. It arises from recognizing that every experience, pleasant or difficult, contributes to our understanding of ourselves and the world.

When purpose is recognized, it becomes possible to appreciate experience itself.

Even moments of pain can reveal truths that might otherwise remain hidden.

This does not mean that difficult experiences become enjoyable. It means we recognize that they still hold value.

For example, when someone loses a loved one, the mind may initially focus on the absence created by the loss. It may say:

I wish I had more time.

This should not have happened.

These thoughts are expressions of expectation and condition.

But another perspective is also possible.

A person can recognize the time that was shared. The moments that were experienced. The love that existed.

When the mind shifts its attention in this way, something remarkable happens.

Instead of being consumed by what is missing, the mind becomes thankful for what was present.

This is the beginning of unconditional thankfulness.

Unconditional thankfulness does not erase grief immediately, but it transforms the relationship we have with it.

Grief becomes less about what we have lost and more about recognizing the value of what we experienced.

In this way, thankfulness changes the direction of awareness.

Instead of moving toward resentment, the mind begins moving toward appreciation.

This shift has a powerful effect on the next stage of the process.

When a person becomes truly thankful, their **intention** begins to change as well.

Resentment naturally produces harmful or defensive intentions.

But thankfulness produces something very different.

It produces **goodwill**.

The mind begins to move toward understanding rather than blame.

And that movement reveals the next attribute in the process of awareness:

Intention.

CHAPTER 15

Intention

Once thankfulness begins to emerge, the direction of the mind changes in an important way.

Resentment and gratitude cannot exist in the same place at the same time. When resentment dominates, the mind searches for blame, injustice, or loss. But when thankfulness appears, the mind begins to move toward understanding.

This shift affects something deeper than emotion.

It affects **intention**.

Intention is the underlying direction of the mind. It shapes the way we interpret events, the way we treat others, and the way we respond to our experiences.

Many people believe intention is something they consciously decide, but in reality, intention often follows the emotional state of the mind.

When a person is resentful, their intention naturally becomes defensive, judgmental, or hostile. They may try to protect themselves, justify their pain, or prove that something unfair has occurred.

These intentions arise automatically from resentment.

But when thankfulness appears, something different happens.

Gratitude softens the mind. Instead of searching for something to blame, the mind begins searching for meaning and understanding.

This shift transforms intention.

When thankfulness is present, intention begins to move toward **goodwill**.

Goodwill is the desire for understanding, peace, and connection rather than conflict.

This is why the type of thankfulness we practice matters.

If thankfulness is conditional—meaning it only appears when circumstances meet our expectations—then intention remains unstable. When conditions are not satisfied, resentment returns and intention becomes ill-willed again.

But when thankfulness becomes **unconditional**, something remarkable occurs.

Intention becomes **automatically good-willed**.

There is no longer a need to force kindness or understanding. The mind naturally moves toward them because it is no longer fighting reality.

In this way, intention reveals the direction awareness is moving.

If intention is driven by resentment, the mind remains trapped in resistance.

If intention is guided by thankfulness, the mind begins moving toward peace.

This insight shows that intention is not simply a moral choice.

It is a reflection of the internal state of awareness. When a person becomes unconditionally thankful for their experiences, their intention aligns naturally with goodwill.

And when goodwill becomes the foundation of intention, the mind becomes ready for the next step in the process.

Because goodwill makes something possible that resentment never allows.

It makes **acceptance** possible.

Acceptance is the moment when the mind stops resisting reality.

And when acceptance appears, the entire relationship with experience begins to change.

CHAPTER 16

Acceptance

When intention becomes guided by goodwill rather than resentment, the mind reaches an important turning point.

This turning point is called **acceptance**.

Acceptance is often misunderstood. Many people believe acceptance means approving of difficult circumstances or pretending that painful experiences are acceptable. But acceptance does not mean agreement, approval, or passivity.

Acceptance means recognizing reality exactly as it is.

It is the moment when the mind stops fighting what has already occurred.

Resistance, on the other hand, is the refusal to acknowledge reality. It is the mind's attempt to argue with events that have already happened.

The mind says:

This should not have happened.

Things should be different.

Reality should match my expectations.

But no amount of resistance can change what has already occurred.

Resistance only creates internal conflict.

Acceptance removes that conflict.

It allows the mind to recognize a simple truth:

Reality exists independently of our expectations.

Once this truth is seen clearly, the struggle between expectation and reality begins to dissolve.

Acceptance does not remove the experience itself. The circumstances remain exactly as they are. But acceptance changes the relationship we have with them.

Instead of fighting reality, we begin to understand it.

This shift creates space within the mind.

When resistance disappears, the mind becomes calmer, clearer, and more open to insight.

In many ways, acceptance is the doorway through which awareness enters.

Without acceptance, the mind remains trapped in cycles of resentment, blame, and denial.

But when acceptance appears, something remarkable becomes possible.

The mind becomes capable of **understanding**.

Understanding is not simply intellectual knowledge. It is the recognition of how and why our experiences unfold the way they do.

Acceptance creates the clarity necessary for that recognition to occur.

It allows us to see the role expectations, conditions, and interpretations play in shaping our emotional experiences.

Without acceptance, the mind remains too busy fighting reality to learn from it.

With acceptance, the mind becomes free to observe.

And observation leads to insight.

This is why acceptance is such a powerful attribute within the process of awareness.

It transforms experience from something we struggle against into something we can learn from.

Once the mind accepts reality, it becomes ready for the next step in the journey toward awareness.

That step is **understanding**.

Understanding reveals the deeper process through which emotions, expectations, and choices interact.

And when that process becomes clear, something extraordinary happens.

We begin to recognize the truth of our own choices.

CHAPTER 17

Understanding

When acceptance appears, the mind becomes quiet enough to observe something it could not see before.

Without resistance, the mind is no longer trying to force reality to match its expectations. Instead, it begins to examine the experience itself.

This examination leads to the next attribute in the process of awareness:

Understanding.

Understanding is more than simply learning information. It is the moment when a person sees clearly how their mind participates in the creation of their emotional experience.

Many people live their lives believing that emotions are caused entirely by external events.

When something painful happens, they assume the emotion must follow automatically.
But when acceptance allows the mind to observe its own process, a deeper truth becomes visible.

Between every event and every emotional experience lies something powerful.

Choice.

Understanding reveals that the mind moves through a sequence when it encounters an experience.

First, the mind interprets the event. It compares the circumstance to its expectations and conditions.

If the circumstance does not satisfy those expectations, resistance appears. Resistance produces emotions such as sadness, anger, resentment, or grief.

But once a person becomes aware of this process, something changes.

They recognize that the interpretation itself is not fixed.

It is chosen.

This realization marks the beginning of true awareness.

When a person understands that expectation creates resistance, and resistance creates emotional suffering, they begin to see that another direction is possible.

Instead of demanding that reality change, they can choose to change their relationship with reality.

This choice does not alter the event itself.

But it transforms the meaning the mind gives to the event.

When the mind recognizes this, something profound occurs.

A person becomes aware that their experience is not determined solely by circumstances.

It is shaped by the choices they make within those circumstances.

This realization is what many traditions describe as **enlightenment**.

Not enlightenment as a mystical escape from life, but enlightenment as the recognition of something that was always present:
the power of choice.

When understanding reaches this level, the mind no longer feels trapped by circumstances. Instead, it begins to see that every experience contains an opportunity to choose how awareness will respond.

This understanding changes the way we view both ourselves and others.

We begin to see that people often act from misunderstanding rather than intention to harm. They are responding to their expectations, their conditions, and their interpretations of reality.

This recognition softens judgment and opens the door to the next attribute in the process of awareness.

Once a person understands the role expectation and choice play in human experience, something naturally follows.

Forgiveness.

Forgiveness becomes possible because we recognize that everyone is navigating the same process of expectation, interpretation, and choice.
When we see this clearly, resentment begins to lose its foundation.

And in its place, a deeper form of compassion begins to emerge.

That compassion leads directly to the next attribute in the journey toward awareness.

Forgiveness.

Part 2 — The Transformation

CHAPTER 18

Forgiveness

When understanding becomes clear, something important begins to change in the way we see both ourselves and others.

Understanding reveals that many of the emotions people struggle with—sadness, anger, resentment, and grief—do not arise simply from events. They arise from the expectations and conditions the mind places on those events.

Once this becomes visible, blame begins to lose its power.

Instead of seeing others as the cause of our suffering, we begin to recognize the deeper process that created the experience.

This realization opens the door to the next attribute in the movement toward awareness:
Forgiveness.

Forgiveness is often misunderstood. Many people believe forgiveness means excusing harmful behavior or pretending that painful experiences did not occur.

But forgiveness is not about denying reality.

Forgiveness is about releasing the expectation that the past should be different than it was.

The past cannot be changed.

No amount of anger, regret, or resentment can alter what has already happened. Holding onto these emotions only extends the suffering created by the original event.

Forgiveness ends that extension.

It is the moment when the mind stops demanding that the past be rewritten.

When a person truly understands the role expectation plays in emotional suffering, forgiveness becomes a natural response.
They see that their own pain often came from holding onto the belief that something should have been different.

And they begin to recognize that others are often acting from the same misunderstanding.

People respond to life through the lens of their own expectations, fears, and interpretations.

Many harmful actions are not the result of deliberate cruelty but the result of confusion, fear, or pain.

Understanding this does not erase the consequences of those actions, but it changes how we hold them within our minds.

Instead of carrying resentment, we release it.

Forgiveness frees the mind from the burden of constantly reliving the past.

But forgiveness does not only apply to others.

It also applies to ourselves.

Many people carry deep regret about decisions they have made, words they have spoken, or actions they wish they could undo.

These regrets often come from holding the expectation that we should have known more or done better in the past.

But the truth is that every person acts according to the level of understanding they had at the time.

Once this becomes clear, self-forgiveness becomes possible.

We recognize that we were learning, just as everyone else is learning.

And when we forgive both ourselves and others, something remarkable happens.

The mind becomes lighter.

The weight of resentment disappears.

In that space, a deeper emotion begins to emerge.

That emotion is not based on conditions, expectations, or judgment.

It is something far more stable and enduring.

It is **unconditional love**.

Forgiveness clears the path that allows unconditional love to appear.

It removes the barriers created by blame, resentment, and regret.

And when those barriers fall away, the final attribute of awareness becomes visible.

Unconditional Love.

CHAPTER 19

Unconditional Love

When forgiveness is complete, something extraordinary becomes possible.

The mind is no longer carrying resentment toward the past. It is no longer demanding that reality satisfy conditions or expectations.

In that freedom, a deeper experience begins to appear.

This experience is **unconditional love**.

Many people believe love is something that depends on circumstances. They believe love must be earned, maintained, or protected. In this view, love becomes conditional. It exists only when certain expectations are fulfilled.

But conditional love is unstable.

When conditions are satisfied, love appears. When conditions are violated, love fades and resentment replaces it.

This type of love is closely tied to expectation.

Unconditional love is different.

Unconditional love does not depend on circumstances being perfect. It does not require reality to satisfy personal expectations.

Instead, unconditional love arises when a person becomes fully thankful for the experience of life itself.

When expectations dissolve, appreciation remains.

This appreciation is not limited to pleasant experiences. It includes the difficult ones as well, because those experiences have contributed to understanding, growth, and awareness.

Unconditional love is the recognition that every experience—joyful or painful—has played a role in revealing truth.

When this realization appears, resentment no longer has a place to exist.

Grief, sadness, and anger may still arise briefly as natural human responses, but they no longer dominate awareness. The mind no longer clings to the expectation that life must unfold differently.

Instead, it becomes thankful for the experience that was given.

This is why unconditional thankfulness naturally leads to unconditional love.

When a person becomes unconditionally thankful for their experiences, their intention becomes good-willed automatically. Acceptance becomes natural. Understanding becomes clear. Forgiveness becomes possible.

All of the attributes begin to align.

Unconditional love is not simply the final attribute in the process.

It is the **center** around which all the other attributes move.
Purpose reveals the meaning within experience.

Thankfulness opens the mind to appreciation.

Intention guides the direction of awareness.

Acceptance releases resistance.

Understanding reveals the role of choice.

Forgiveness frees the mind from resentment.

And when these attributes work together, unconditional love emerges naturally.

At this point, something profound becomes visible.

Peace does not come from controlling life.

Peace comes from recognizing the choice available within every experience.

This realization is what many traditions refer to as enlightenment.

Not enlightenment as something mystical or unreachable, but enlightenment as the simple recognition of the truth that has always been present.

Closing Insight

We exist to choose.

Every moment presents an opportunity to choose how we interpret our experiences, how we respond to our circumstances, and how we relate to the world around us.

When this choice becomes clear, awareness changes.

And when awareness changes, peace becomes possible.

True peace is not something we wait for life to provide.

It is something that appears when we recognize the power of our own choice.

This is the realization at the heart of the Seven Attributes.

And once it is seen clearly, one final question remains.

Will you be honest with yourself about the choice you are making?

Part IV — Awareness Through Experience

CHAPTER 20

The Nature of Experience

Experience is one of the most familiar realities in human life, yet it is rarely examined closely.

Every person lives through experiences every day. We speak to others, remember the past, anticipate the future, feel emotions, form judgments, and respond to circumstances. Because this happens constantly, experience can seem obvious. It can appear to be nothing more than life unfolding moment by moment.

But when experience is observed carefully, something deeper becomes visible.

Experience is not merely what happens.

Experience is what happens **as it is encountered by awareness**.

This distinction is important. Events occur in the world continually, but events do not become experience until they are perceived, interpreted, and felt by the individual. The same circumstance can produce very different experiences in different people, not because reality itself has changed, but because the relationship to that reality is different.

One person may encounter delay and feel frustration. Another may encounter the same delay and feel patience. One may experience criticism as rejection. Another may experience it as guidance. One may see loss only as absence. Another may eventually see within that same loss a reason for thankfulness.

The event may be the same.

The experience is not.

This reveals something essential.

Experience is not created by circumstance alone. It is created through the meeting of circumstance and interpretation.

What happens in the external world matters, but it is not the only factor. The mind is always participating. It brings memory, expectation, meaning, fear, desire, belief, and attention into every moment. These shape the way an event is received.

Because of this, experience is never purely external.

It is relational.

It is the relationship between reality and the mind that encounters it.

This is why experience becomes the proper place to begin any serious examination of self-awareness. If we do not understand the nature of experience, we may believe that our emotions are caused entirely by the world outside us. We may believe peace depends on circumstances becoming favorable. We may assume suffering exists only because life has failed to give us what we wanted.

But when we begin to understand experience more clearly, another possibility appears.

We begin to see that much of human suffering is not found only in events themselves, but in the way the mind relates to events.

This does not mean circumstances are meaningless, nor does it deny the reality of pain, loss, or difficulty. Rather, it means that experience contains more than the event alone. It also contains the interpretation of the event.

And where interpretation exists, awareness becomes possible.

This is what makes experience so important.

Experience is not just the setting of life. It is the field in which awareness is revealed.

Within experience, expectations become visible. Emotions arise. Meanings are formed. Choices appear. Peace or resistance begins to take shape. The entire movement of awareness is contained within the way a person experiences life.

For this reason, experience is not something to move past too quickly. It is something to observe.

When observed honestly, experience begins to teach.

It teaches us what we value. It teaches us what we fear. It teaches us what we are expecting. It reveals the conditions we place on life and the meanings we assign to what happens. It shows us whether we are moving toward acceptance or resistance, toward understanding or resentment, toward forgiveness or toward the continuation of conflict.

In this sense, experience is not just something we have.

It is something through which we come to know ourselves.

Every experience carries the potential for awareness because every experience reveals something about the relationship between the mind and reality. Even painful experiences can become instructive when they are examined clearly. What first appears as frustration may reveal expectation. What first appears as sadness may reveal resistance to what is. What first appears as peace may reveal the release of that resistance.

Experience is therefore one of the great teachers of human life.

Not because every experience is pleasant, but because every experience contains information.

It shows us how awareness is moving.

This is why Experiology places such importance on experience. Experience is not treated as random or meaningless. It is the place where the structure of awareness becomes visible. It is where the individual can begin to see how emotions form, how interpretations develop, and how choices shape the direction of inner life.

When this becomes clear, experience is no longer something to fear or avoid.

It becomes something to learn from.

It becomes the place where awareness deepens.

And once that is understood, a person can begin to approach life differently. Instead of asking only, *What happened to me?* they may begin asking, *How am I experiencing what happened?*

That question changes everything, because it shifts attention from circumstance alone to the living process through which circumstance becomes meaningful.

It is in that process that self-awareness begins.

CHAPTER 21

Emotion as a Signal

Emotion is one of the most immediate parts of human experience.

It appears quickly, often before we have time to think about what is happening. A word is spoken, a situation changes, an unexpected event occurs, and emotion follows almost instantly. Joy, frustration, sadness, anger, relief, fear, or gratitude can arise before we fully understand why they have appeared.

Because emotions can feel so powerful, many people assume that emotions are the cause of their experience. They believe their feelings are created directly by the events that occur around them.

But when emotion is examined carefully, something else becomes visible.

Emotion is not the cause of experience.

Emotion is the signal of experience.

It signals that something within the mind has encountered a difference between expectation and reality.

When life unfolds exactly as the mind expected, emotion may remain calm or unnoticed. But when reality diverges from expectation, the mind reacts.

It says:

This should not be happening.

This should have happened differently.

This should not have ended this way.

When expectation meets a reality it cannot control, emotion appears.

In this way, emotion becomes an indicator. It reveals that the mind has formed a condition about how life should be unfolding.

Sadness appears when we expect a circumstance to be different than it actually is.

Frustration appears when reality refuses to follow the plans we created.

Anger appears when we believe something has violated what we believe should be true.

In each case, emotion reveals something about the relationship between expectation and reality.

This realization changes the way emotion is understood.

Instead of seeing emotions as enemies that must be controlled or suppressed, we begin to see them as information.

Emotion shows us where expectation exists.

And once expectation becomes visible, awareness becomes possible.

Emotion therefore plays an important role in the development of self-awareness.

It points toward the very place where the mind has created a condition that reality cannot satisfy.

When this is recognized, emotion stops being something we must fight against.

Instead, it becomes something we can learn from.

It becomes a signal that invites us to look more closely at the expectations we are holding and the choices we are making.

And when we begin to listen to that signal, the process of awareness can begin.

CHAPTER 22

Reflection and Awareness

Once emotion reveals that expectation is present, the next step becomes possible.

Reflection.

Reflection is the moment when the mind pauses long enough to observe what is happening within it.

Instead of reacting immediately, the mind begins to look inward. It asks questions about the experience that is unfolding.

Why am I feeling this way?

What expectation did I hold?

What condition did I believe life should satisfy?

Reflection slows the process of reaction and allows awareness to appear.

Without reflection, emotions often move directly into reaction. A person may become angry and immediately speak harsh words. They may feel sadness and withdraw without understanding why.

They may feel resentment and hold onto it for years without ever examining the expectation that created it.

But reflection interrupts that automatic process.

It creates space.

In that space, awareness can grow.

Through reflection, the mind begins to notice the expectations that shape its emotional experience. It begins to see how often it compares reality to an image of how life should have been.

This observation is the beginning of awareness.

Awareness does not require perfect understanding or flawless behavior. It simply requires the willingness to observe what is happening honestly.

When the mind becomes capable of observing itself, something powerful occurs.

It becomes possible to see the difference between the event itself and the interpretation the mind has created about that event.

And once that difference becomes clear, another possibility appears.

Choice.

Reflection reveals that the mind is not trapped inside its emotional reactions. It reveals that emotional experience is influenced by the expectations we carry and the meanings we assign to what happens.

When this becomes visible, awareness begins to grow.

And as awareness grows, the mind gains the ability to respond differently to the experiences life presents.

CHAPTER 23

The Path of Resistance

When expectation remains unexamined, the mind often moves in a predictable direction.

It moves toward resistance.

Resistance occurs when the mind insists that reality should be different than it is. It is the internal struggle that arises when life refuses to satisfy the conditions we have created.

Resistance can appear in many forms.

It may appear as anger when someone behaves differently than we expected.

It may appear as resentment when circumstances do not reward our efforts.

It may appear as sadness when life changes in ways we did not want.

In each case, resistance grows from the same source.

Expectation.

The mind compares reality to an image of how things should have been. When that image is not fulfilled, resistance begins.

This resistance can become exhausting. The mind fights against events that have already happened. It demands that life undo something that cannot be undone.

But reality continues to move forward, unaffected by the expectations we hold.

When resistance dominates awareness, emotional conflict grows. The mind becomes trapped in cycles of frustration, disappointment, and blame.

And because the expectation remains, the emotional experience continues.

Resistance does not solve the conflict.

It sustains it.

Understanding the path of resistance is important because it reveals how easily the mind can become trapped inside expectations that reality cannot satisfy.

But once resistance becomes visible, another path becomes possible.

CHAPTER 24

The Path of Awareness

The alternative to resistance is awareness.

Awareness begins when the mind recognizes the expectations it has created and becomes willing to release them.

Instead of demanding that life follow a particular plan, awareness begins to observe what is actually happening.

This shift may appear small, but it changes the entire experience of life.

When expectation dissolves, resistance fades.

When resistance fades, the mind becomes calmer.

Events that once triggered strong emotional reactions begin to appear differently. Instead of asking why something should not have happened, the mind begins asking what can be understood from the experience.

Purpose becomes visible.

Thankfulness becomes possible.

Acceptance replaces struggle.

Understanding begins to grow.

And forgiveness becomes easier.

These movements are the same attributes described earlier in the book.

They appear naturally when the mind releases its demand that reality be different than it is.

Awareness does not eliminate difficulty from life.

Loss will still occur.

Unexpected events will still appear.

But awareness changes how those experiences are held.

Instead of fighting them, the mind begins to understand them.

And in that understanding, peace begins to appear.

CHAPTER 25

Recognizing Expectations

At the center of this entire process lies one simple ability.

The ability to recognize expectation.

Expectations often operate quietly within the mind. They shape our interpretations of events without announcing themselves clearly.

We expect people to behave in certain ways.

We expect circumstances to unfold according to our plans.

We expect life to follow the path we imagined.

When these expectations remain invisible, emotions can feel confusing and overwhelming. A person may feel sadness, anger, or frustration without fully understanding why those emotions appeared.

But when expectations become visible, the experience begins to change.

Instead of focusing only on the event, the mind begins to notice the condition it created about that event.

It begins to see the expectation that life should have been different.

This recognition is powerful because it reveals the true source of the emotional tension.

The tension does not come only from the event itself.

It comes from the difference between the event and the expectation.

Once this becomes clear, the mind gains the opportunity to release the expectation and accept reality as it is.

When this happens, resistance fades and peace becomes possible.

Recognizing expectations therefore becomes one of the most important skills in self-awareness.

It allows us to see the connection between expectation, emotion, and peace.

And once that connection becomes clear, the same truth appears again and again within every experience.

We always have a choice.

We can continue holding the expectation that reality should be different.

Or we can release that expectation and move toward awareness.

The direction we choose determines the path our experience will take.

Toward resistance.

Or toward peace.

CHAPTER 26

Why We Exist

For as long as human beings have been aware of themselves, they have asked a question that seems impossible to answer.

Why do we exist?

Philosophers, religions, and scientists have offered many explanations. Some say life exists to serve a higher purpose. Others say existence is the result of natural processes without deeper meaning.

But when we examine our direct experience, something very simple becomes visible.

Every moment of life involves one activity.

Choice.

From the moment we wake until the moment we fall asleep, our lives are filled with decisions.

Some choices are obvious. We decide what to say, what to do, where to go, and how to respond to situations around us.

Other choices are quieter and less visible.

We choose how to interpret events.

We choose how to respond to emotions.

We choose whether to hold onto resentment or move toward understanding.

Even in moments when we believe we are not choosing, the mind is still making decisions.

It interprets experiences, forms judgments, and directs our awareness in one direction or another.

In this way, life itself can be understood as a continuous movement of choice.

If this is true, then emotions begin to appear in a different light.

Rather than viewing emotions as random reactions, we can see them as signals that reveal the direction of our choices.

When the mind holds expectations and conditions, emotions such as sadness, anger, and resentment appear.

When the mind releases those conditions and moves toward acceptance and thankfulness, emotions such as peace and love appear.

Emotions allow us to experience the direction our awareness has taken.

They show us whether we are moving toward resistance or toward understanding.

This perspective reveals something profound about human existence.

Emotions are not obstacles to awareness.

They are guides.

They allow us to feel the consequences of our choices.

Without emotion, choice would exist only as an intellectual idea.

Emotion allows us to experience it directly.

Through emotion we learn what expectation feels like.

Through emotion we learn what acceptance feels like.

Through emotion we learn what resentment feels like.

And through emotion we learn what unconditional love feels like.

In this way, emotions become part of the process through which awareness develops.

They allow us to recognize the direction our mind is moving and adjust our choices accordingly.

This leads to a powerful realization.

Perhaps the purpose of life is not simply to achieve certain outcomes or accumulate experiences.

Perhaps the deeper purpose of life is to become aware of the choices we are making.

When awareness recognizes those choices clearly, something extraordinary becomes possible.

We begin to understand the connection between expectation, emotion, and peace.

And when that understanding becomes complete, we see the truth that has been present all along.

We exist to choose.

Every moment of life presents an opportunity to choose how awareness will move.

Toward resistance.

Or toward understanding.

Toward resentment.

Or toward unconditional love.

Life will continue to present experiences.

But the direction those experiences take within us will always depend on one thing.

The choice we make.

CHAPTER 27

Grief

Grief is often described as one of the most powerful emotions a human being can experience.

It arrives when something deeply meaningful is lost. The absence left behind can feel overwhelming, and many people believe grief is simply an unavoidable response to that loss.

But when grief is examined carefully, it reveals something deeper about the human mind.

Grief is not only the experience of loss.

It is also the experience of expectation.

When someone we love is no longer present, the mind immediately forms a condition. It expects the circumstance to be different than it actually is.

It says:

This should not have happened.
I should have more time.

Life should be different than this.

These thoughts are expressions of the same principle that appears in sadness.

They are expectations that reality cannot fulfill.
And when those expectations collide with reality, the mind experiences the emotional weight we call grief.

This understanding does not mean grief is unimportant or insignificant. On the contrary, grief reveals how deeply we care about the people and experiences in our lives.

But grief also contains something else.

It contains an opportunity to see the truth within the experience.

When grief first appears, the mind often focuses on the absence created by loss. It focuses on what is no longer available.

But another perspective is possible.

A person can recognize the time that was shared. The experiences that were lived. The love that existed during that time.

When the mind shifts in this way, the experience begins to transform.

Instead of focusing on the time that no longer exists, the mind becomes thankful for the time that was given.

This is where unconditional thankfulness begins to appear.

Unconditional thankfulness does not require the circumstance to change. It does not demand that life reverse itself or satisfy expectations.

It simply recognizes the value of what was experienced.

When this recognition appears, grief begins to lose its hold on the mind.

The experience is no longer defined only by loss.

It becomes defined by appreciation.

In this moment, something remarkable becomes visible. Love remains.

Not conditional love that depends on circumstances continuing forever, but unconditional love for the experience itself.

This is why grief can become a powerful teacher.

It reveals the difference between expectation and acceptance.

It shows us the conditions we place on life.

And it presents the opportunity to choose a different relationship with reality.

When expectation dissolves, appreciation becomes possible.

When appreciation appears, unconditional love remains.

Grief, in this way, can become the doorway through which awareness deepens.

It reveals the truth hidden within one of life's most difficult experiences.

The truth that even in moments of loss, something meaningful still exists.

The love that was experienced.

And the realization that we were given the opportunity to experience it at all.

This realization does not erase the memory of loss.

But it transforms the way we carry it.

Instead of carrying grief alone, we carry love.

And that love becomes part of the awareness that guides us forward.

CHAPTER 28

The Test

Ideas are easy to understand when life is calm.

Concepts about awareness, acceptance, and peace can appear clear when circumstances are comfortable and predictable. Many people believe they understand these ideas simply because they make sense intellectually.

But true understanding is revealed only when life becomes difficult.

Every insight must eventually face a test.

For me, that test arrived in the form of grief.

Before that moment, I had already begun to understand the Seven Attributes. I had observed the relationship between expectation, emotion, and awareness. I had recognized that sadness was the expectation for the circumstance to be different than it actually is.

The idea made sense.

But an idea alone does not prove itself.

Life eventually presents an experience powerful enough to challenge what we believe we understand.

When that moment arrived, I was confronted with one of the deepest emotions a human being can experience—grief.

The loss was sudden and overwhelming. The weight of sadness, sorrow, and disbelief appeared all at once.

In that moment, the mind naturally moved toward expectation.

It wanted the circumstance to be different.

It wanted time to reverse itself.

It wanted reality to change.

This is the point where many people become trapped inside grief. The expectation remains, and because reality cannot satisfy it, the emotional experience continues.

But something had already begun to change within me. I remembered the realization that had come years earlier when I first asked a simple question:

What is grief?

The answer that appeared was unexpected.

Grief, sorrow, and sadness are the expectation for the circumstance to be different than it actually is.

At the time, that realization was only an idea.

But now it was standing directly in front of me as an experience.

In that moment I had a choice.

I could continue holding the expectation that reality should be different.

Or I could release the expectation and accept the experience exactly as it was.

This was the moment when the Seven Attributes were no longer theoretical.

They became something real.
I chose thankfulness.

Instead of focusing on the time that was no longer available, I became thankful for the time that had been given.

I became thankful for the moments that had been shared, the memories that would never fade, and the love that had existed during that time.

As soon as thankfulness appeared, something changed.

My intention became good-willed automatically.

Acceptance followed.

Understanding appeared.

And forgiveness emerged—not only toward others, but toward myself for ever believing that the experience should have been different than it was.

In that moment, unconditional love became visible.

Not love based on conditions or expectations, but love based on appreciation for the experience itself.

The grief did not disappear instantly, but it transformed.

It was no longer defined by resentment or expectation.

It became an expression of love.

This experience revealed something that could not be understood intellectually alone.

The Seven Attributes were not just ideas.

They were a process through which awareness could move even in the most difficult moments of life.

The experience became proof that the realization was true.

Even in the deepest grief, peace remained possible.

But peace appeared only when one thing became clear.

The choice.

Life had presented the most powerful emotional experience imaginable.

And within that experience, the same truth remained.

Peace could only be found through the recognition of my choice.

That moment revealed something I will never forget.

The Seven Attributes were not created by the experience.

They were confirmed by it.

And through that confirmation, the truth became undeniable.

Peace is always available when we recognize the choice we have.

CHAPTER 29

The Simplicity

One of the most interesting things about the Seven Attributes is how people respond when they first hear them.

Some people understand immediately.

Others become confused.

And many people say the same thing:

It seems too simple.

Human beings often expect profound truths to be complicated. We assume that understanding life must involve complex systems, difficult practices, or years of study.

Because of this expectation, simplicity can be difficult to recognize.

But many of the most important truths in life are simple.

They are simple not because they are shallow, but because they describe something fundamental about how reality works.

The Seven Attributes describe one of these simple truths.

Sadness is the expectation for the circumstance to be different than it actually is.

Once this is seen clearly, many emotional experiences begin to make sense. We begin to notice how often the mind compares reality to its expectations.

When reality does not match those expectations, resistance appears.

Resistance produces emotional tension.

But when the expectation disappears, the tension disappears as well.

The simplicity of this realization can feel surprising because it reveals something that has always been present.

It shows that many of the struggles we experience come from the conditions we place on life.

These conditions often appear so natural that we never question them.

We assume life must meet our expectations in order for us to feel at peace.

But once we recognize this pattern, another possibility appears.

Peace does not require life to change.

Peace requires our relationship with life to change.

This is where the Seven Attributes begin to function together.

They are not complicated instructions. They are observations about how awareness moves.

Purpose allows us to see that experiences can teach us something.

Thankfulness shifts our focus from what is missing to what was given.
Intention moves toward goodwill when gratitude appears.

Acceptance releases the struggle against reality.

Understanding reveals the role expectation plays in emotional experience.

Forgiveness frees the mind from holding onto the past.

And unconditional love becomes the center that allows all of these attributes to exist together.

When people first hear this process, they often expect something more complicated.

But the truth is that awareness does not require complexity.

It requires honesty.

It requires the willingness to look directly at our own expectations and recognize how they influence our emotions.

This honesty can be uncomfortable at first, because it reveals something we might not have noticed before. It reveals that we participate in the creation of our emotional experience.

But it also reveals something empowering.

If expectations create suffering, then releasing those expectations creates freedom.

And once that freedom is experienced, the simplicity of the realization becomes clear.

The Seven Attributes are not difficult to understand.

They are simply difficult to see when the mind is focused on expecting life to be different than it is.

But once the mind becomes aware of this pattern, something changes.

The truth becomes obvious.

And when the truth becomes obvious, the path toward peace becomes much clearer.

Because the process was never complicated.

It was always simple.

We only needed to see it.

Part V — Living the Awareness

CHAPTER 30

The Mirror of the Mind

Once a person becomes familiar with the Seven Attributes, something interesting begins to happen.

The mind becomes easier to observe.

Instead of being carried away by emotions without understanding them, a person can begin to watch how their awareness moves from moment to moment.

In many ways, the Seven Attributes become a mirror.

They reflect the direction the mind is taking.

When awareness is moving toward peace, the attributes begin to appear naturally. A person recognizes purpose in their experience. Thankfulness begins to replace resentment. Intention moves toward goodwill. Acceptance becomes possible. Understanding grows.

Forgiveness emerges. And unconditional love becomes visible.

But when awareness moves in the opposite direction, the reflections appear instead.

Purpose becomes **no purpose**.

Thankfulness becomes **conditional thankfulness**.

Good intention becomes **ill intention**.

Acceptance becomes **denial**.

Understanding becomes **not understanding**.

Forgiveness becomes **not forgiving**.

Unconditional love becomes **conditional love**.

These reflections do not appear because someone is failing or doing something wrong. They appear because the mind is responding to experience through expectation.

Expectation creates resistance.

Resistance creates emotional conflict.

When the mind becomes caught in that conflict, it begins to move through the reflections rather than the attributes.

This is why awareness is so important.

When a person can observe their own mind clearly, they begin to recognize which direction their awareness is moving.

They can see whether resentment or thankfulness is guiding their interpretation.

They can notice whether they are accepting reality or denying it.

They can recognize whether they are holding onto blame or moving toward forgiveness.

This observation changes everything.

Without awareness, emotions can feel overwhelming and uncontrollable. A person may feel trapped in them without understanding why they exist.

But when the mind begins to observe itself, emotions become signals rather than obstacles.

They reveal something important.

They reveal the direction awareness has taken.

If resentment appears, it often means expectation is still present.

If peace appears, it often means expectation has been released.

This insight turns emotional experience into something valuable.

Instead of fearing difficult emotions, we can learn from them.

They become indicators that guide awareness back toward understanding.

The Seven Attributes function as a map that helps us navigate this process.
They allow us to see where our awareness currently stands and where it can move next.

In this way, the mind becomes both the observer and the observed.

It becomes capable of watching its own patterns and adjusting the direction it takes.

This is one of the most powerful aspects of self-awareness.

It allows us to step outside automatic reactions and become conscious participants in our own experience.

And when that happens, something remarkable becomes possible.

The mind becomes free to choose the direction awareness will move.

Toward resistance.

Or toward peace.
The mirror of the mind simply reveals the truth of where we currently stand.

And once that truth is visible, the next step always remains available.

The choice.

CHAPTER 31
Living the Attributes

Understanding the Seven Attributes is one thing.

Living them is another.

Ideas can be understood quickly, but real transformation happens only when those ideas become part of everyday life.

The Seven Attributes are not meant to remain concepts inside a book. They are meant to become tools for awareness that can be used in real moments, with real emotions, and real experiences.

Life constantly presents situations that challenge our expectations.

A conversation may not go the way we hoped. A plan may fail. Someone we care about may act in a way we did not expect.

In those moments, the mind automatically begins to interpret what is happening.

Expectation appears.

Conditions form.

And emotions begin to follow.

This is the point where awareness becomes valuable.

Instead of reacting automatically, a person can pause and observe what the mind is doing.

Is the mind demanding that the situation be different?

Is it forming expectations that reality must satisfy?

If so, the path of resistance has begun.

But awareness offers another possibility.

A person can ask a simple question:

What attribute is available right now?

Perhaps the situation can reveal purpose.
Perhaps it offers an opportunity for thankfulness.

Perhaps it invites acceptance rather than resistance.

Perhaps it requires forgiveness.

Each experience becomes an opportunity to practice awareness.

This does not mean that emotions disappear immediately.

Human emotions are natural and will always arise.

But the Seven Attributes allow us to work with those emotions rather than become trapped by them.

Over time, this practice begins to change the way we experience life.

Situations that once produced frustration become opportunities for understanding.

Conflicts that once created resentment become opportunities for forgiveness.
Losses that once created only sadness begin to reveal appreciation for the time that was shared.

Gradually, awareness begins to replace automatic reaction.

The mind becomes calmer.

Emotions become clearer.

And peace becomes more consistent.

Living the attributes does not require perfection.

It requires practice.

There will be moments when expectation returns and resistance appears again.

But every moment also contains a new opportunity to recognize what is happening and choose a different direction.

This is the beauty of awareness.

It does not demand that we never struggle.
It simply invites us to see the struggle clearly.

And when we see it clearly, we remember something important.

We always have another choice.

The Seven Attributes are not rules.

They are reminders.

They remind us that within every experience, awareness has the opportunity to move toward peace.

And the more often we recognize that opportunity, the more naturally the attributes begin to guide our lives.

Eventually, awareness becomes less of an effort and more of a way of being.

Life continues to present challenges.

But the mind responds differently.

It responds with understanding, with forgiveness, and with unconditional love.

And in that way, the Seven Attributes become something more than a model.

They become a way of living.

CHAPTER 32

The Moment of Honesty

Every insight described in this book eventually leads to one simple moment.

A moment of honesty.

The Seven Attributes explain how awareness moves. They show the relationship between expectation, emotion, and peace. They reveal how resistance forms and how acceptance dissolves it.

But understanding these ideas intellectually is not enough.

For awareness to truly appear, a person must be willing to look at themselves honestly.

This moment of honesty is where real transformation begins.

When a difficult emotion appears—sadness, resentment, anger, or grief—the mind often looks outward for explanations. It may blame circumstances, other people, or events that feel unfair.

This reaction is natural.

But awareness invites a different question.

Instead of asking *Who or what caused this emotion?*, we begin asking something deeper.

What expectation am I holding right now?

This question changes the direction of attention.

Instead of focusing only on the external event, the mind begins to examine its own conditions.

It begins to see how it expected the situation to unfold differently.

It begins to notice the internal demand that reality should be something other than what it is.

This is the moment when honesty becomes important.

Because it can be uncomfortable to admit that the mind is holding expectations that reality cannot satisfy. It is often easier to believe the world is responsible for our emotional state.

But when we are honest with ourselves, something powerful becomes visible.

We see the connection between expectation and the emotion we are experiencing.

Once that connection becomes clear, the Seven Attributes begin to guide the mind toward a different response.

Purpose reminds us that the experience may have something to teach.

Thankfulness reminds us that something valuable may still exist within the moment.

Intention begins to move toward goodwill.

Acceptance releases the demand that reality must change.

Understanding reveals the role of expectation.

Forgiveness frees us from resentment.
And unconditional love becomes possible.

But none of this can happen without honesty.

Honesty is the doorway through which awareness enters.

Without it, the mind remains convinced that its expectations are justified and necessary.

With honesty, those expectations begin to dissolve.

When they dissolve, resistance disappears.

And when resistance disappears, peace becomes visible.

This moment of honesty may seem small, but it is one of the most important moments in the entire process of awareness.

It is the moment when we stop avoiding the truth and begin to see it clearly.

And once the truth is seen clearly, something remarkable happens.

The mind becomes free to choose a different direction. That is why awareness ultimately leads back to the same question again and again.

A question that only each individual can answer for themselves.

Will you be honest with yourself?

CHAPTER 33

The Invitation

By now you have seen the pattern.

Sadness appears when expectation demands that reality be different than it actually is.

Resistance grows when those expectations remain.

But awareness reveals another direction.

The Seven Attributes describe that direction.

They show how the mind moves from resistance toward peace.

Purpose allows us to see that experience can teach us something.

Thankfulness allows us to appreciate what has been given.

Intention moves toward goodwill.

Acceptance releases the struggle against reality.

Understanding reveals the role of expectation.

Forgiveness frees the mind from the past.

And unconditional love becomes the center from which awareness grows.

These attributes are not rules that must be followed perfectly.

They are simply observations about how awareness works.

Every human being encounters the same process.

Every person experiences expectations.

Every person experiences emotions that follow those expectations.

And every person is presented with the same opportunity.

The opportunity to recognize the choice within their experience.
This book does not claim to remove difficulty from life.

Loss will still occur.

Challenges will still arise.

Life will continue to change in ways we cannot predict.

But awareness changes the way we meet those experiences.

Instead of resisting them, we begin to understand them.

Instead of demanding that life be different, we begin to accept what is.

Instead of focusing on what is missing, we begin to appreciate what was given.

And in that appreciation, something remarkable appears.

Peace.

Not the fragile peace that depends on perfect circumstances, but the stable peace that exists when expectations dissolve.
The Seven Attributes are not something that belong to one person or one idea.

They belong to anyone who is willing to observe their own experience honestly.

They belong to anyone who is willing to recognize the moment when expectation appears.

And they belong to anyone who is willing to choose awareness instead of resistance.

This book is not meant to be the end of a journey.

It is an invitation.

An invitation to look at your own experiences with greater awareness.

An invitation to recognize the expectations that shape your emotions.

An invitation to see the choice that exists within every moment.

Because once that choice becomes visible, everything begins to change.
Life continues exactly as it always has.

But the way we experience life becomes different.

And when that happens, the realization at the center of this book becomes clear.

True peace does not come from controlling life.

True peace comes from recognizing the power of your choice.

The Seven Attributes simply reveal the path that leads to that recognition.

The rest is up to you.

What will you choose?

Figure 1– The Seven Attributes Model

Part VI — The Experiology Models

CHAPTER 34

The Seven Attributes Model

Throughout this book, the Seven Attributes have been described as a process the mind moves through when it encounters experience.

While these ideas can be understood through reading, they can also be seen visually through what can be called **The Seven Attributes Model**.

The model represents the relationship between the attributes and the way awareness moves between them.

At the center of the model is **unconditional love**.

Unconditional love is not placed at the center by accident. It represents the natural state that appears when expectation, resentment, and resistance have dissolved. When the other attributes begin to align, unconditional love becomes visible.

Around the center are the attributes that guide awareness toward that state.

These attributes form a structure that reflects the natural movement of the mind:

Purpose
Thankfulness
Intention
Acceptance
Understanding
Forgiveness

Each of these attributes represents a step in the process of awareness.

Purpose allows us to recognize that experiences may contain meaning.

Thankfulness shifts our attention from what we have lost to what was given.

Intention moves awareness toward goodwill rather than resentment.

Acceptance releases the struggle against reality.

Understanding reveals the relationship between expectation and emotion.

Forgiveness frees the mind from resentment toward both the past and ourselves.

When these attributes work together, unconditional love naturally appears.

The model shows that these attributes are not isolated ideas.

They function as a system.

When one attribute begins to appear, the others often follow naturally. Thankfulness encourages goodwill. Goodwill encourages acceptance. Acceptance opens the door to understanding. Understanding makes forgiveness possible.

Eventually, the mind arrives at unconditional love.

But the model also reveals something equally important.

Each attribute has a reflection.

If the mind moves in the opposite direction, the attributes transform into their opposites.

Purpose becomes **no purpose**.

Thankfulness becomes **conditional thankfulness**.

Intention becomes **ill intention**.

Acceptance becomes **denial**.

Understanding becomes **not understanding**.

Forgiveness becomes **not forgiving**.

Unconditional love becomes **conditional love**.

The model therefore illustrates two directions awareness can move.

One direction leads toward peace.

The other leads toward resistance.

Every experience places us somewhere within this movement.

When expectation dominates the mind, the reflections appear.

When awareness recognizes expectation and releases it, the attributes begin to emerge.

This is why the model is useful.

It provides a way to visualize what is happening internally during emotional experiences.

Instead of feeling lost inside emotions, a person can recognize where their awareness currently stands within the process.

They can ask:

Am I moving toward resentment or toward thankfulness?

Toward denial or toward acceptance?

Toward blame or toward forgiveness?

The model does not judge these movements.

It simply reveals them.
And once the direction becomes visible, the most important part of the process appears again.

The opportunity to choose.

The Seven Attributes Model therefore serves as a map of awareness.

It reminds us that every experience contains two possible directions.

And it reminds us that peace appears when awareness begins to move toward the attributes rather than their reflections.

Because at the center of that movement, something always remains.

Unconditional love.

Figure 2– Resistance vs Awareness Chart

CHAPTER 35

Resistance vs Awareness

Throughout this book, two different directions of the mind have been described.

One direction moves toward **resistance**.

The other moves toward **awareness**.

Every emotional experience we have follows one of these two paths.

When the mind holds expectations and conditions, resistance appears. The mind begins to reject reality and demand that circumstances be different than they actually are.

This rejection creates tension.

That tension becomes what we experience as emotional suffering.

Sadness, resentment, anger, and grief often arise when the mind insists that reality must change in order for peace to exist.

This is the path of resistance.

On this path, the reflections of the attributes begin to appear.

The mind may believe the situation has **no purpose**.

It may feel **conditional thankfulness**, believing it can only appreciate life when certain expectations are satisfied.

Its intention may become **ill-willed**, searching for blame or injustice.

It may fall into **denial**, refusing to accept what has already occurred.

It may remain in **not understanding**, unable to see the role expectation plays in the emotional experience.

It may hold onto resentment through **not forgiving**.

And eventually, love becomes **conditional**, existing only when circumstances meet certain demands.

This path creates conflict because reality rarely satisfies every expectation the mind creates.

But there is another direction available.

This is the path of awareness.

Awareness begins when the mind recognizes the expectation it is holding.

Instead of demanding that reality change, the mind begins to observe its own reaction.

This observation opens the door to the Seven Attributes.

The mind begins to see **purpose** within experience. It becomes **thankful** for what was given rather than focused only on what was lost.

Its **intention** moves toward goodwill.

It allows **acceptance** to replace resistance.

It develops **understanding** of how expectation creates emotional tension.

It moves toward **forgiveness**, releasing resentment toward both others and itself.

And from this process, **unconditional love** appears.

These two directions—resistance and awareness—exist within every human experience.

The difference between them is not determined by the event itself.

It is determined by the relationship the mind has with the event.

If expectation controls the mind, resistance follows.

If awareness recognizes expectation, the attributes begin to appear.

The Resistance vs Awareness model exists to illustrate this movement.

It reminds us that every emotional experience is pointing to one of these directions.

Either the mind is resisting reality.

Or the mind is learning from it.

And once this becomes visible, the same truth continues to appear again and again.

Within every experience, there is a moment where the direction can change.

That moment is the recognition of choice.

And once the choice is seen clearly, the mind becomes free to move toward awareness instead of resistance.

Figure 3– Awareness Spiral

CHAPTER 36

The Awareness Spiral

Awareness rarely appears all at once.

For most people, understanding grows gradually over time. Experiences repeat themselves in different forms, and each time they appear, the mind has another opportunity to see something more clearly.

This movement of learning can be understood as **the Awareness Spiral**.

Unlike a straight line, a spiral moves forward while also circling back around familiar points. We encounter similar emotions, similar challenges, and similar expectations more than once in our lives.

At first, these repeated experiences can feel frustrating. A person may wonder why the same types of difficulties keep appearing.

But the spiral reveals that these experiences are not exactly the same each time.

Each time the experience appears, awareness has the opportunity to deepen.

For example, the first time a person encounters disappointment, they may react entirely through expectation and resistance.

The emotion may feel overwhelming, and they may believe the circumstance itself is responsible for their suffering.
Later in life, a similar experience may occur again.

But this time something is different.

The person may begin to recognize the expectation that is forming in their mind. They may notice the condition they are placing on reality.

This recognition changes the experience.

The emotion may still appear, but awareness begins to understand it.

As the spiral continues, each new experience becomes an opportunity to move further toward understanding.

Purpose becomes easier to see.

Thankfulness begins to appear more naturally.

Intention moves more consistently toward goodwill.

Acceptance becomes quicker.

Understanding deepens.

Forgiveness becomes easier.

And unconditional love becomes more stable.

The spiral shows that awareness is not about achieving perfection.

It is about **growing in clarity over time**.

There will still be moments when expectation appears suddenly and resistance follows. But with awareness, those moments do not last as long.

The mind recognizes the pattern more quickly.

It remembers the choice more quickly.

And it returns to peace more easily.

Each turn of the spiral represents a deeper level of understanding.

The same lessons appear again, but they are seen from a higher level of awareness.

In this way, life becomes a process of continual learning.

Experiences are not simply obstacles to overcome. They are opportunities to deepen awareness.

The Awareness Spiral reminds us that growth does not move in a straight line.

It moves in cycles of experience, reflection, and understanding.

And with each cycle, awareness expands.

As awareness expands, the Seven Attributes become easier to recognize.

Eventually, what once felt confusing begins to feel simple.

The patterns become clear.

The emotions become understandable.

And the choice becomes visible more quickly.

The spiral therefore represents something hopeful.

It shows that awareness can continue to deepen throughout life.

Every experience contains the opportunity to move further along the spiral.

Every moment contains the opportunity to recognize the truth that has been present all along.

The truth that peace becomes available whenever we recognize the choice before us.

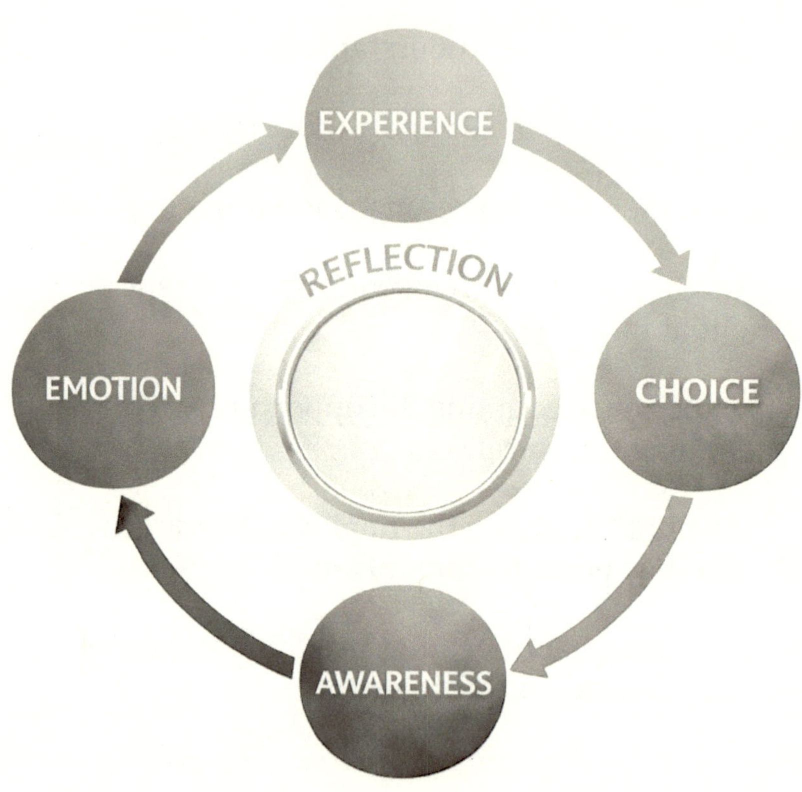

Figure 4– Reflection Diagram

CHAPTER 37

The Reflection

As awareness grows, the mind begins to notice a pattern.

Every movement toward peace has a reflection that moves in the opposite direction.

The Seven Attributes reveal the path toward awareness, but each of these attributes also has an opposite expression. These opposites form what can be called **the reflection of awareness**.

The reflection shows what happens when expectation and condition remain in control.

When the mind does not recognize expectation, awareness moves through the reflections rather than the attributes.

The reflections appear as follows:

Purpose reflects **No Purpose**

Thankfulness reflects **Conditional Thankfulness**

Good Intention reflects **Ill Intention**

Acceptance reflects **Denial**

Understanding reflects **Not Understanding**
Forgiveness reflects **Not Forgiving**

Unconditional Love reflects **Conditional Love**

These reflections do not represent failure or weakness. They represent the natural direction the mind moves when expectation dominates awareness.

For example, when a difficult experience occurs, the mind may immediately believe the situation has no meaning or value. This is the reflection of purpose.

When expectations are not satisfied, thankfulness may become conditional. The mind may believe it can only appreciate life when circumstances meet certain conditions.

From there, intention may shift toward frustration or blame. Acceptance may be replaced by denial. Understanding may give way to confusion.

If resentment continues, forgiveness becomes difficult.

Eventually, love itself becomes conditional. It exists only when expectations are satisfied.

This entire movement forms the reflection of awareness.

But just as the mind can move through these reflections, it can also move in the opposite direction.

Awareness allows the mind to recognize expectation.

When expectation is seen clearly, the attributes begin to appear.

Purpose replaces the belief that experience has no meaning.

Thankfulness replaces resentment.

Good intention replaces blame.

Acceptance replaces denial.

Understanding replaces confusion.

Forgiveness replaces resentment.

And unconditional love replaces conditional love.

The reflection therefore shows that every experience contains two possible directions.

The mind can move toward resistance.

Or it can move toward awareness.

This realization becomes powerful because it allows us to observe our own state of mind without judgment.

Instead of asking whether we are right or wrong, we can simply ask:

Which direction is my awareness moving?

If resentment appears, we can recognize that expectation may still be present.

If peace appears, we can recognize that awareness has moved toward the attributes.

The reflection makes the process visible.

It allows us to see the patterns of the mind as they unfold.

And once those patterns are visible, something important becomes clear.

We are not trapped inside them.

Because at every point within the reflection, the same opportunity exists.

The opportunity to choose a different direction.

The opportunity to move toward awareness.

And the opportunity to return once again to the center of the model.

Where unconditional love remains available.

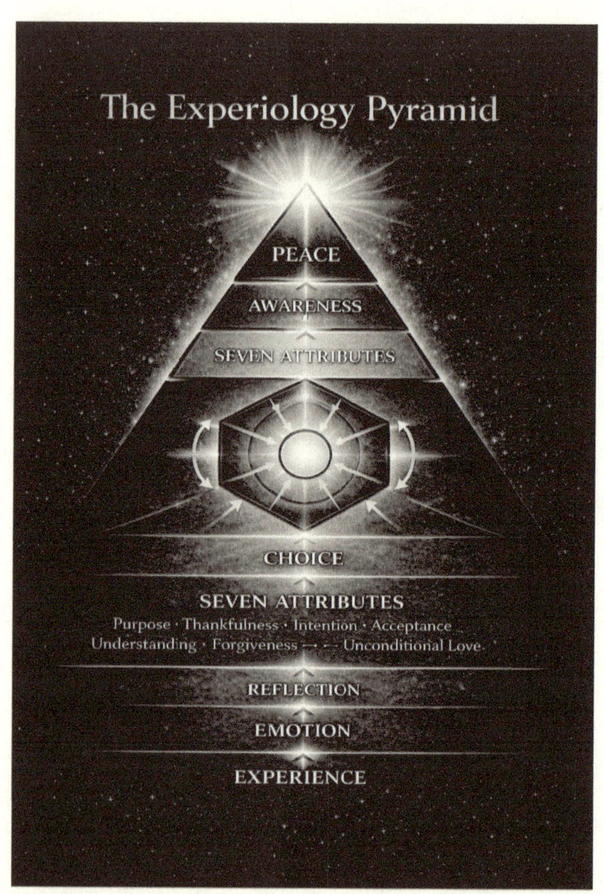

Figure 5 — The Experiology Pyramid illustrates the ascending movement of awareness through the Seven Attributes.

CHAPTER 38

The Experiology Pyramid

The Experiology Pyramid is a visual model that represents the ascending movement of awareness through the Seven Attributes. While the Seven Attributes can be understood individually, the pyramid shows that they also function as a progression. Each level builds upon the one before it, moving the mind from the basic recognition of experience toward the highest expression of awareness.

The pyramid is important because it reveals that awareness is not random. It develops in a recognizable direction.

At the base of the pyramid is **Purpose**.

Purpose is the beginning because awareness cannot grow if experience is seen as meaningless. When a person believes their pain, struggle, or difficulty has no purpose, the mind often moves toward resistance. But when purpose is recognized, experience changes.

The mind begins to see that even difficult circumstances may contain something to learn, reveal, or understand. Purpose does not remove pain, but it gives the experience a place within awareness.

From purpose, the pyramid rises to **Thankfulness**.

Once purpose is recognized, thankfulness becomes possible. Thankfulness does not mean a person must enjoy every experience. It means they begin to recognize value within what has been given. Even in difficulty, something may still be seen, learned, remembered, or appreciated. Thankfulness shifts awareness away from what is missing and toward what has been present. This movement is essential because resentment cannot dominate the mind when genuine thankfulness appears.

Above thankfulness is **Intention**.

Intention is the direction awareness chooses to move. Once a person recognizes purpose and becomes thankful, the question naturally becomes: how will I now relate to this experience? Intention determines whether awareness will move toward goodwill or toward harm, toward openness or toward defensiveness. It is the attribute that gives direction to the mind.

Without intention, awareness remains passive. With intention, awareness begins to act deliberately.

From intention, the pyramid rises to **Acceptance**.

Acceptance is one of the most important movements in the entire process. It is the release of the struggle against reality. The mind often suffers because it continues to demand that life be different than it is. Acceptance does not mean approval of every event, nor does it mean passivity. It means recognizing reality as it is rather than fighting what has already occurred. When acceptance appears, resistance begins to dissolve. The mind stops exhausting itself by arguing with reality.

Above acceptance is **Understanding**.

Understanding is what emerges when the mind begins to see clearly. It recognizes the role of expectation, condition, and interpretation in emotional experience. Understanding reveals why suffering has formed and how awareness can move differently. It is more than information. It is insight. A person may know many ideas intellectually, but understanding means they begin to see those ideas operating within their own mind and life.

Through understanding, awareness becomes stable and less easily overwhelmed by immediate emotion.

From understanding, the pyramid rises to **Forgiveness**.

Forgiveness becomes possible when understanding deepens. Without understanding, forgiveness can feel unnatural or impossible. The mind holds onto blame because it remains attached to hurt, expectation, and judgment. But when understanding appears, the person begins to see more clearly how suffering has formed in themselves and in others. Forgiveness is not forgetting or pretending nothing happened. It is the release of the burden of continuing to carry resentment. It frees awareness from the past and allows the mind to move forward without being defined by injury.

At the top of the pyramid is **Unconditional Love**.

Unconditional love is the highest point because it is the fullest expression of awareness. It is love that is no longer dependent on conditions being met. It does not

say, "I will love only if life goes according to my expectations." It is not controlled by circumstance, reward, or convenience.

Unconditional love becomes possible when purpose has been recognized, thankfulness has appeared, intention has been directed toward good, acceptance has released resistance, understanding has revealed truth, and forgiveness has freed the mind from resentment.

In this way, unconditional love is not separate from the other attributes. It is what naturally appears when the attributes align.

The pyramid shows that awareness rises. It begins with the recognition that experience has purpose and moves upward through gratitude, direction, acceptance, understanding, and forgiveness until it reaches the highest form of relating to life.

This structure also shows why the attributes cannot be treated as isolated ideas. Each one supports the next.

Purpose opens the mind.
Thankfulness softens it.
Intention directs it.
Acceptance steadies it.
Understanding clarifies it.
Forgiveness frees it.
Unconditional love fulfills it.

The Experiology Pyramid therefore represents more than a hierarchy. It represents the upward movement of consciousness through experience.

When a person is trapped in expectation, resentment, or resistance, awareness tends to remain low and unstable. But as the Seven Attributes begin to operate, the mind rises. It becomes less controlled by conditions and more aligned with peace.

This is why the pyramid is so important in Experiology.

It shows that peace is not reached through force. It is reached through the development of awareness.

And it shows that the highest state of awareness is not simply knowledge.

It is love without condition.

The Experiology Symbol

Figure 5 — The Experiology Symbol

CHAPTER 39

The Experiology Symbol

The Experiology Symbol represents the structure of awareness described throughout this book. While the Seven Attributes and the Experiology Framework explain the process of self-awareness through words and ideas, the symbol expresses that same process visually. It is a representation of how experience, emotion, reflection, and choice interact within the movement of awareness.

At the center of the symbol is a simple truth:

Experience.

Experience is the foundation of human life. Every moment we live becomes an experience that we perceive, interpret, and respond to. Experience is not merely what happens in the external world; it is the relationship between the event and the mind that encounters it. Because of this relationship, experience becomes the starting point of awareness.

Surrounding experience is **Emotion**.

Emotion is the immediate response that signals how the mind is relating to what has occurred. As described earlier, emotion is not simply a reaction to events. It is a signal that reveals the presence of expectation or acceptance within the mind. When expectation collides with reality, emotions such as sadness, anger, or frustration appear. When expectation dissolves and acceptance appears, emotions such as peace, appreciation, and love emerge.

Emotion therefore acts as a guide. It tells us something about the direction our awareness has taken.

The next movement in the symbol is **Reflection**.

Reflection is the moment when awareness turns inward and observes what is happening within the mind. Instead of reacting automatically, reflection allows a person to examine their expectations, interpretations, and emotional responses. Through reflection, the process of awareness becomes visible.

Without reflection, emotions simply move into reaction. But when reflection appears, a person can begin to see the relationship between expectation, emotion, and experience.

Reflection reveals something that is often hidden.

It reveals **choice**.

Choice is the final movement represented within the symbol. Once the mind recognizes the expectations it is holding and the emotions those expectations create, it becomes possible to choose how awareness will move next.

A person may continue holding the expectation and remain in resistance.

Or they may release the expectation and move toward acceptance, understanding, forgiveness, and unconditional love.

This moment of choice exists within every experience.

The Experiology Symbol illustrates this entire process as a continuous cycle.

Experience leads to emotion.
Emotion invites reflection.
Reflection reveals choice.
Choice determines how the next experience will be interpreted.

Because life continues to present new experiences, the process repeats again and again. Each moment provides another opportunity to observe, reflect, and choose the direction awareness will take.

The circular movement of the symbol reflects this ongoing nature of awareness. Self-awareness is not a single realization that occurs once and never returns. It is a living process that unfolds continuously through experience.

At any moment, the cycle may move toward resistance or toward awareness.

When expectation dominates the mind, the cycle produces emotional conflict and resistance. But when reflection reveals expectation and choice is exercised honestly, the cycle begins to move toward peace.

In this way, the Experiology Symbol represents more than a diagram. It represents the structure of conscious experience itself.

It shows that awareness develops through the interaction of experience, emotion, reflection, and choice.

And it reminds us of the truth that lies at the center of Experiology.

Every experience contains the opportunity for awareness.

And within that awareness, the power to choose always remains.

CHAPTER 40

The Practice

Understanding an idea is not the same as living it.

Throughout this book, the nature of experience, emotion, reflection, and choice has been explored. The Seven Attributes have been described as a path toward awareness, and the Experiology models have illustrated the structure of that process. These ideas can be understood intellectually, but awareness does not develop through understanding alone.

Awareness develops through practice.

The practice of Experiology does not require complicated techniques or rigid disciplines. It begins with something far simpler.

Observation.

Life constantly presents experiences. Conversations occur, plans change, emotions appear, and unexpected events unfold. In most cases, these moments pass quickly because the mind reacts automatically.

It interprets events according to its expectations, and emotion follows immediately.

But when a person begins to practice awareness, something changes.

Instead of reacting immediately, the mind pauses.

It observes the experience as it is happening.

This small moment of observation creates space within the mind. In that space, the process described throughout this book becomes visible.

An experience has occurred.

An emotion has appeared.

Now reflection becomes possible.

Reflection allows the mind to ask questions that normally go unnoticed.

What expectation did I hold in this moment?
Why did this emotion appear?
What condition did I believe life should satisfy?

These questions are not meant to judge the experience or force a particular emotional response.

They simply reveal the relationship between expectation and emotion.

Once expectation becomes visible, the next step appears naturally.

Choice.

Choice is the point where awareness becomes active. Instead of continuing the automatic reaction created by expectation, a person can decide how they will now relate to the experience.

This is where the Seven Attributes become practical tools.

In any experience, a person can ask simple questions:

Is there purpose in this experience?

Is there something I can be thankful for?

What intention will guide my response?

Am I accepting reality as it is, or resisting it?

What am I beginning to understand about this moment?

Is forgiveness possible here?

Can unconditional love exist within this experience?

These questions gently guide awareness toward the attributes rather than toward resistance.

Over time, this practice changes the way the mind responds to life.

Situations that once created frustration begin to reveal meaning. Moments that once produced resentment begin to reveal opportunities for forgiveness. Experiences that once felt meaningless begin to reveal purpose.

This does not mean that difficult emotions will disappear entirely.

Human beings will always experience sadness, disappointment, anger, and grief. These emotions are part of the human condition. The practice of awareness does not eliminate emotion.

Instead, it changes the way emotion is understood.

Emotion becomes a signal.

It reveals the expectations that the mind is holding and invites reflection about whether those expectations can truly be satisfied by reality.

When expectation dissolves, resistance dissolves with it.

And when resistance dissolves, peace becomes possible again.

The practice of Experiology therefore does not ask a person to control life. It asks them to observe their relationship with life.

It asks them to notice the expectations that shape their emotional experience.

And it invites them to recognize the choice that exists within every moment.

Each time awareness appears, the practice becomes easier.

Observation becomes more natural.

Reflection becomes quicker.

Choice becomes clearer.

Eventually, the Seven Attributes begin to operate quietly within awareness itself. Purpose becomes easier to see. Thankfulness becomes more natural. Acceptance becomes more consistent. Understanding deepens. Forgiveness becomes lighter. And unconditional love becomes the center from which awareness moves.

At that point, the practice no longer feels like effort.

It becomes a way of living.

Life will continue to present experiences as it always has. Unexpected events will occur. Loss will still exist. Plans will still change.

But awareness transforms the way those experiences are held.

Instead of reacting automatically, the mind begins to observe, reflect, and choose.

And each time that choice is recognized, the same truth becomes clear again.

Peace does not come from controlling life.

Peace comes from recognizing the power of your choice.

Closing Section

The Seven Statements of Awareness

The Seven Attributes describe the movement of awareness through experience.
Each attribute reveals a different way the mind can relate to life when expectation is replaced by understanding.

These attributes can be summarized through seven simple statements.

They are not rules to follow or beliefs that must be accepted.
They are reminders of how awareness can move when the mind becomes honest about its expectations and the choices it is making.

Purpose

Every experience has the potential to reveal something.

When awareness looks closely, even difficulty can teach, clarify, and guide the mind toward understanding.

Purpose does not mean every event is pleasant.
It means every experience can contribute to awareness.

Thankfulness

Thankfulness recognizes what has been given.

Instead of focusing only on what is missing or what did not happen as expected, thankfulness acknowledges the value that existed within the experience.

It transforms resentment into appreciation.

Intention

Intention determines the direction awareness will move.

A person may respond to life with resentment and defensiveness, or with goodwill and openness.

Intention reveals the path awareness chooses to follow.

Acceptance

Acceptance releases the struggle against reality.

It does not require approval of every circumstance, but it recognizes that resisting what has already occurred cannot change it.

When acceptance appears, the mind becomes free to respond rather than react.

Understanding

Understanding reveals the relationship between expectation, emotion, and experience.

It allows the mind to see how its interpretations influence its emotional responses.

With understanding, awareness becomes clearer and less controlled by automatic reactions.

Forgiveness

Forgiveness releases the weight of resentment.

It frees the mind from carrying the past forward into every new experience.

Forgiveness does not erase what happened.
It simply removes the need to continue holding the burden of it.

Unconditional Love

Unconditional love is the highest expression of awareness.

It is love that does not depend on circumstances being perfect or expectations being satisfied.

It recognizes the value of experience itself.

Together, these seven statements describe the path awareness follows when expectation dissolves and understanding appears.

The Experiology Manifesto

Human beings spend much of their lives searching for peace.

They look for it in success, security, relationships, possessions, and achievement.
They believe peace will arrive when life finally becomes the way they hoped it would be.

But experience reveals something different.

Life does not always follow our expectations.

Plans change.
Loss occurs.
Unexpected events appear.

When peace depends on life unfolding exactly as we imagined, peace becomes fragile.

Experiology begins with a simple observation:

Many of the emotions we experience arise from the expectation that reality should be different than it actually is.

When the mind demands that circumstances change in order for peace to exist, resistance appears.

But when expectation dissolves, something remarkable happens.

The mind becomes free.

Experiology does not attempt to control life.

It seeks to understand the relationship between experience, emotion, reflection, and choice.

It recognizes that awareness grows when we observe our expectations honestly and acknowledge the choices we are making within each experience.

Through this awareness, the Seven Attributes appear.

Purpose reveals meaning within experience.
Thankfulness recognizes what was given.
Intention guides the direction of awareness.
Acceptance releases resistance.
Understanding reveals truth.

Forgiveness frees the mind from the past.
Unconditional love becomes the highest expression of awareness.

Experiology is not a belief system or doctrine.

It is an observation about how awareness develops within human experience.

It suggests that peace is not created by controlling life.

Peace appears when we recognize the role our expectations play in shaping our emotional experience and when we choose awareness instead of resistance.

In this way, Experiology is not about escaping life.

It is about understanding it.

The Foundational Principle of Experiology

At the center of Experiology lies a simple principle.

Emotion reveals the relationship between expectation and reality.

When the mind expects circumstances to be different than they are, resistance appears and emotions such as sadness, frustration, or anger follow.

When expectation dissolves and reality is accepted as it is, peace becomes possible.

This principle does not deny the complexity of human life.
Loss, uncertainty, and difficulty will always exist.

But it reveals that our emotional experience is influenced not only by events themselves but by the expectations we place upon those events.

When expectation is recognized, awareness appears.

When awareness appears, choice becomes visible.

And when choice becomes visible, the direction of experience can change.

This principle forms the foundation of the entire Experiology framework.

Experiology Glossary

Awareness
The ability to observe one's own thoughts, emotions, and expectations clearly.

Experience
The interaction between external events and the mind that perceives them.

Emotion
A signal that reveals the relationship between expectation and reality.

Reflection
The act of observing one's thoughts, interpretations, and emotional responses.

Choice
The ability to determine how awareness will respond to an experience.

Expectation
A condition created by the mind about how reality should unfold.

Resistance
The emotional conflict that arises when expectation demands that reality be different than it is.

Acceptance
The recognition of reality as it is without resisting what has already occurred.

The Seven Attributes
Purpose, Thankfulness, Intention, Acceptance, Understanding, Forgiveness, and Unconditional Love.

Experiology
The study of experience and awareness through the relationship between expectation, emotion, reflection, and choice.

Gratitude

At the heart of the Seven Attributes lies a quiet realization.

Life itself is a gift.

This realization may seem obvious at first, but many people move through life without fully recognizing it. The mind often becomes focused on what is missing, what should have happened, or what still needs to be achieved.

Expectation pulls attention toward what reality has not provided.

But awareness brings attention back to what has already been experienced.

Gratitude begins in this recognition.

When we pause long enough to observe our lives honestly, we begin to see the countless moments that have shaped who we are.

Conversations, relationships, lessons, challenges, joys, and even the difficulties that forced us to grow.

Each experience becomes part of the story of our awareness.

Gratitude does not mean that every moment of life is easy or pleasant.

Life contains pain, loss, and uncertainty.

But gratitude allows us to see that even these experiences have contributed to our understanding.

They have shaped the perspective we hold today.

They have revealed the expectations we carried.

And they have guided us toward the awareness we now possess.

In this way, gratitude becomes something deeper than appreciation for pleasant events.

It becomes appreciation for **the experience of life itself**.

When we look at life through this lens, resentment begins to fade.

Instead of focusing only on what we believe should have happened, we begin to recognize what was given.

Moments of love.

Moments of learning.

Moments of connection.

Moments that will remain part of our awareness forever.

Gratitude transforms the way we see our past.

It allows us to appreciate the time we were given rather than mourn only the time we wish we had.

It allows us to see the lessons hidden within difficulty.

And it allows us to recognize that every experience, whether joyful or painful, has played a role in shaping our awareness.

This is why gratitude holds such an important place within the Seven Attributes.

Thankfulness opens the door to goodwill.

Goodwill leads to acceptance.

Acceptance allows understanding.
Understanding makes forgiveness possible.

And forgiveness clears the way for unconditional love.

In this way, gratitude quietly connects all of the attributes together.

It reminds us that life is not something we control.

Life is something we experience.

And within that experience, something meaningful remains.

The opportunity to learn.

The opportunity to grow.

And the opportunity to recognize the gift of being here at all.

When this realization becomes clear, gratitude becomes natural.

Not forced.

Not conditional.

But unconditional.

A quiet appreciation for the simple truth that we were given the opportunity to experience life.

And within that experience, we were given something even more valuable.

The ability to choose.

The Gift of Experience

When we look back over the journey described in this book, one truth begins to stand out.

Life is not simply a series of events.

Life is a series of **experiences**.

Every moment we live becomes part of our awareness. Some experiences bring joy and connection. Others bring challenge, loss, and uncertainty. Yet all of them contribute to the way we understand ourselves and the world around us.

The mind often separates experiences into two categories: good and bad.

Pleasant experiences are welcomed.

Difficult experiences are resisted.

But when awareness deepens, something interesting begins to happen.

This separation begins to dissolve.

We begin to see that even the most difficult experiences can contain meaning.

They reveal our expectations.

They expose the conditions we place on life.

And they show us how our minds respond when those expectations are not fulfilled.

Without these experiences, many of these patterns would remain hidden.

In this way, experience itself becomes a teacher.

The joyful moments show us what connection and appreciation feel like.

The difficult moments show us where expectations still exist.

Both are valuable.

Both contribute to awareness.

This realization changes the way we view life.

Instead of asking why certain experiences occurred, we begin to ask what they reveal about our awareness.

Instead of resisting every difficulty, we begin to look for the understanding hidden within it.

Over time, this perspective transforms the way we relate to our own lives.

We begin to see that every experience—pleasant or painful—has shaped the person we are today.

Every conversation, every relationship, every moment of joy, every moment of grief has contributed to the awareness we now possess.

When we see life through this lens, gratitude becomes easier.

Not gratitude only for the comfortable moments, but gratitude for the full range of experiences that have guided us toward understanding.

This does not mean we seek difficulty or suffering.

It simply means we recognize the value of what has already occurred.

Every experience we have lived has helped reveal the process described in the Seven Attributes.

They have shown us how expectation forms.

They have shown us how resistance appears.

And they have shown us how awareness can transform our relationship with reality.

When this becomes clear, something important changes.

Instead of wishing that our lives had unfolded differently, we begin to appreciate the experiences that shaped us.

They become part of the story of our awareness.

And within that story, something meaningful appears.

The recognition that life itself is the opportunity.

The opportunity to experience.
The opportunity to learn.

And the opportunity to choose.

Because every experience, no matter how simple or profound, contains the same possibility.

The possibility of awareness.

And through awareness, the possibility of peace.

The Seven Attributes to Self Awareness

A Final Summary

Human experience is guided by expectation.

When the mind expects the circumstance to be different than it actually is, resistance appears.

That resistance is what we experience as sadness, grief, anger, and resentment.

Sadness is the expectation for the circumstance to be different than it actually is.

Expectation creates conditions.

When those conditions are not satisfied, emotional suffering follows.

But awareness reveals another direction.

Purpose allows us to see that experience can teach us something.

Thankfulness allows us to appreciate what was given.

Intention moves awareness toward goodwill.

Acceptance releases the struggle against reality.

Understanding reveals the role expectation plays in emotion.

Forgiveness frees the mind from resentment toward the past.

And unconditional love becomes visible when expectation dissolves.

These attributes reveal a simple truth about human life.

We are constantly presented with experiences.

Within each experience, a choice exists.

We can resist reality.

Or we can become aware of it.

Peace appears when we recognize that choice.

True peace is attained through the recognition of your choice.

And the most important question remains:

Will you be honest with yourself?

A Question for the Reader

Throughout this book, one idea has appeared again and again.

Life presents experiences.

From those experiences, emotions arise.

When we look closely, those emotions often reveal the expectations we hold about how life should unfold.

When those expectations are not satisfied, resistance appears.

But awareness reveals something important.

Within every experience, there is a moment that is often overlooked.

A moment of reflection.

And within that moment, something powerful becomes visible.

Choice.

The choice is not about controlling life or forcing circumstances to become what we want them to be.

Life will continue to change.
Unexpected events will occur.
People will act in ways we did not predict.

But within every experience, we still encounter a decision.

We can hold onto the expectation that reality should be different than it is.

Or we can observe that expectation and choose a different relationship with the experience.

We can move toward resistance.

Or we can move toward awareness.

The Seven Attributes were never meant to be a system that tells you what to believe.

They are simply a way of helping you see what is already happening within your own experience.

They help reveal the moment when expectation appears.

They help reveal the emotions that follow.

And they help reveal the choice that exists within every moment of awareness.

The question that remains is not theoretical.

It is personal.

It appears quietly in the moments when life does not unfold the way we hoped.

In those moments, you may pause and ask yourself something simple.

What expectation am I holding right now?

And once that expectation becomes visible, another question naturally follows.

What will I choose?

The Final Reflection

At the beginning of this book, a question was asked.

What is sadness?

The answer that followed was simple.

Sadness is the expectation for the circumstance to be different than it actually is.

At first, this realization may seem small. It may even seem too simple. But when we begin to examine our experiences honestly, its meaning becomes clearer.

Expectation creates conditions.

Conditions demand that life unfold in a certain way.

When reality does not satisfy those conditions, resistance appears.

That resistance becomes what we experience as sadness, resentment, frustration, and grief.

The Seven Attributes reveal another direction.

Purpose allows us to recognize that experiences can teach us something.

Thankfulness shifts our attention from what we believe we have lost to what we were given.

Intention moves awareness toward goodwill.

Acceptance releases the struggle against reality.

Understanding reveals the relationship between expectation and emotion.

Forgiveness frees the mind from resentment toward the past.

And unconditional love becomes the center from which awareness grows.

Together, these attributes reveal something that has always existed within every human experience.

The presence of choice.

Life will continue to present moments that challenge our expectations.

Loss will occur.

Circumstances will change.

Events will unfold in ways we could never predict.

But within every experience, something remains constant.

The opportunity to recognize the choice within the moment.

When expectation controls the mind, resistance follows.

When awareness recognizes expectation, peace becomes possible.

This is not a theory.

It is something that can be observed directly within your own experience.

Every emotion you feel can reveal something about the expectations the mind is holding.

Every moment of awareness can reveal the direction the mind is moving.

Toward resistance.

Or toward peace.

This book does not claim to remove difficulty from life.

What it offers is something different.

It offers a way to understand the process taking place within the mind during those difficult moments.

Once that process becomes visible, something powerful becomes clear.

Peace is not something that arrives when life becomes perfect.

Peace appears when expectation dissolves.

And when expectation dissolves, the truth at the center of this book becomes unmistakable.

True peace is attained through the recognition of your choice.

The Seven Attributes simply reveal the path that leads to that recognition.

The rest belongs to you.

And so the final question remains.

A question that only you can answer.

Will you be honest with yourself about the choice you are making?

Because in the end, the truth remains the same.

We exist to choose.

A Message to the Reader

If you have reached this point in the book, you have traveled through the entire process of the Seven Attributes.

You have explored the nature of experience, the role expectation plays in emotion, and the way awareness can reveal the moment of choice within every situation.

But the true value of these ideas is not found in the pages of this book.

It is found in your own experience.

The purpose of the Seven Attributes is not to persuade you to believe something new. It is to help you observe something that has always been present in your life.

Every day, life will continue to present experiences.

Some of those experiences will bring joy, connection, and understanding. Others will bring difficulty, loss, or uncertainty.

This is the nature of being human.

What matters is not that these experiences occur.

What matters is how we relate to them.

At times, you may notice expectation forming in the mind. You may notice the quiet belief that life should have unfolded differently. When that expectation appears, emotions will often follow.

But awareness gives you something powerful in that moment.

The ability to pause.

The ability to observe what the mind is doing.

And the ability to recognize the choice that exists within the experience.

This choice does not require perfection.

No one moves through life without moments of frustration, sadness, or resistance. The purpose of awareness is not to eliminate these experiences, but to help us understand them.

When expectation becomes visible, another direction becomes possible.

A person can recognize purpose within the experience.

They can become thankful for what has been given.

They can choose goodwill rather than resentment.

They can accept reality rather than struggle against it.

They can seek understanding rather than confusion.

They can forgive rather than remain attached to the past.

And they can allow unconditional love to remain at the center of awareness.

These movements are what the Seven Attributes describe.

They are not rules.

They are reminders.

Reminders that within every experience there exists an opportunity to see more clearly, to understand more deeply, and to choose more consciously.

The journey of awareness does not end when the final page of this book is reached.

In many ways, it begins there.

Because every moment of life continues to offer the same invitation.

The invitation to observe your experience honestly.

The invitation to recognize the expectations shaping your emotions.

And the invitation to choose the direction awareness will move.

Where that journey leads is something only you can discover.

But one truth remains present in every experience.

Within every moment of awareness, a choice exists.

And that choice will always belong to you.

What will you choose?

An Invitation to Practice

If the ideas in this book have resonated with you, the most meaningful step forward is not to study them further, but to practice observing them within your own life.

Awareness does not grow through theory alone. It grows through experience.

Every day, life will present moments that invite reflection. A conversation may not go as expected. A plan may change. An event may occur that challenges the conditions the mind has quietly placed on reality.

In those moments, the opportunity for practice appears.

You may begin by noticing the emotion that arises. Instead of reacting immediately, pause and observe what is happening within your mind. Ask yourself a simple question:

What expectation am I holding right now?

This question often reveals the condition the mind has created about how life should unfold. When that expectation becomes visible, the Seven Attributes offer a way to respond with awareness rather than resistance.

You may begin to see purpose within the experience, recognizing that even difficult moments can reveal something important. You may become thankful for what was given rather than focusing only on what was missing. Your intention may shift toward goodwill rather than resentment. Acceptance may replace the struggle against reality. Understanding may grow as you observe the connection between expectation and emotion. Forgiveness may free the mind from holding onto the past. And unconditional love may remain at the center of awareness.

These movements are not meant to happen perfectly.

They are meant to be practiced.

At first, the mind may return often to expectation and resistance. This is natural. Awareness develops gradually as we observe our experiences with honesty and patience.

Each moment of reflection strengthens that awareness.

Each moment of awareness reveals the choice within the experience.

Over time, the practice becomes simpler. Instead of reacting automatically, the mind begins to recognize the process unfolding within it. Emotions become signals. Expectations become visible. And the direction of awareness becomes clearer.

Eventually, the Seven Attributes begin to operate quietly in the background of everyday life. Purpose becomes easier to see. Thankfulness appears more naturally. Acceptance replaces struggle. Understanding deepens. Forgiveness becomes lighter. And unconditional love becomes a steady presence within awareness.

This is the true practice of self-awareness.

Not controlling life, but observing how the mind relates to life.

Every experience will continue to offer this opportunity.

The opportunity to notice expectation.

The opportunity to reflect.

And the opportunity to choose the direction awareness will move.

Because within every experience, the same possibility always exists.

The possibility of awareness.

And through awareness, the possibility of peace.

The invitation is simple.

Observe your experience honestly.

Recognize the expectation that appears.

And remember the choice that exists within every moment.

What will you choose?

About the Author

Josiah Lucero is the creator of *The 7 Attributes to Self Awareness* and the founder of the Experiology framework, a model developed through years of reflection, personal experience, and a deep search for understanding.

His work centers on a simple but powerful realization: many of the emotional struggles people experience arise from the expectation that circumstances should be different than they actually are. Through observing this relationship between expectation, emotion, and awareness, Josiah developed the Seven Attributes as a way to help individuals recognize the moment of choice that exists within every experience.

The insights presented in this book were shaped not only by philosophical inquiry but also by life itself. Personal challenges, including profound loss and moments of deep reflection, tested and ultimately confirmed the principles described throughout these pages. Through those experiences, Josiah discovered that even in the most difficult circumstances, peace remains possible when we understand the role expectation plays in shaping our emotional experience.

Today, Josiah shares these ideas through his work in self-awareness education and through the development of the Experiology framework. His message remains grounded in a single guiding principle:

True peace is attained through the recognition of your choice.

Through *The 7 Attributes to Self Awareness*, he invites readers to examine their own experiences, understand the relationship between expectation and emotion, and recognize the choice that exists within every moment of awareness.

www.ingramcontent.com/pod-product-compliance
Lightning Source LLC
LaVergne TN
LVHW100526110826
845146LV00002B/788

* 9 7 9 8 9 9 5 5 0 5 8 0 8 *